# Exercises in the Art of Helping

## Third Edition

**Mark E. Young**
*University of Central Florida*

**Samantha Chromy**
*University of Bristol, England*

PEARSON

Merrill
Prentice Hall

Upper Saddle River, New Jersey
Columbus, Ohio

**Vice President and Executive Publisher:** Jeffery W. Johnston
**Publisher:** Kevin M. Davis
**Development Editor:** Autumn Crisp Benson
**Production Editor:** Mary Harlan
**Design Coordinator:** Diane C. Lorenzo
**Cover Design:** Jason Moore
**Cover Image:** Corbis
**Production Manager:** Laura Messerly
**Director of Marketing:** Ann Castel Davis
**Marketing Manager:** Autumn Purdy
**Marketing Coordinator:** Tyra Poole

**Pearson Prentice Hall™** is a trademark of Pearson Education, Inc.
**Pearson®** is a registered trademark of Pearson plc
**Prentice Hall®** is a registered trademark of Pearson Education, Inc.
**Merrill®** is a registered trademark of Pearson Education, Inc.

Pearson Education Ltd.
Pearson Education Singapore Pte. Ltd.
Pearson Education Canada, Ltd.
Pearson Education–Japan

Pearson Education Australia Pty. Limited
Pearson Education North Asia Ltd.
Pearson Educación de Mexico, S.A. de C.V.
Pearson Education Malaysia Pte. Ltd.

10 9 8 7 6 5 4 3 2 1
ISBN: 0-13-119657-X

# Introduction

Welcome to the Third Edition of *Exercises in the Art of Helping*. This learning guide was originally developed at the suggestion of students who requested more out-of-class practice. In this guide, you will be asked to respond to a variety of client situations as a helper. Because there may be many good ways to respond, not all of your answers will directly correspond with the answers that we give in the back of the study guide. If your answers differ, reflect on the differences and come to a conclusion about what you think is best. If your answers are vastly different, check with your instructor. Your instructor may ask you to turn in the workbook, or just specific pages as you go along.

## Organization
Each chapter in this study guide corresponds to the same-numbered chapter in the text, *Learning the Art of Helping,* Third Edition.  An earlier version of the text will not have the same chapter numbers. If you do not have the text, you can still use this guide and the accompanying CD. Simply review the chapter summary and glossary before you begin.

## Chapter Summary and Glossary
Each chapter begins with a summary of the chapter in the textbook, *Learning the Art of Helping*, Third Edition. In addition, you will find definitions of key terms from the chapter in the glossary. You may want to review these first to remind you of the textbook information before you begin your practice. You can also use these sections to review before a classroom quiz.

## Video Exercises
There are 11 video segments on the accompanying CD. Following this introduction is a list of the segments and the names of each helper. The helpers in the video are working with real people who are dealing with real situations. They are not actors. The dialogue was not scripted but was filmed just as it happened. This means that the helper responses are not perfect. You will certainly see places where you could have done better. At times like this, reflect on what you think a better response might have been.

## Timer
On each segment, you will see a timer in the lower right hand corner of the screen. The timer will help you pinpoint the specific client or helper responses referred to in the exercises. You will use the CD most intensively in chapters 4-10 because this is where the basic or "building-block" skills are presented.

## Written Exercises
You may be tempted just to watch the videos. But like learning a foreign language, you can not just observe, you have to learn to produce a good response. You must interact with the material. In this study guide, most chapters have a Written Exercises section. Writing your answers gives you a little more time to think than when you are actually in a helping session. Therefore, it is a good first step before actual practice. Take a look at our answers to the written and video segment exercises in the back of this study guide. For faster progress, share your responses with fellow students and your teachers and obtain feedback.

**Self-Assessment**

As you learn each of the skills, the Self-Assessment section of each chapter of the study guide asks you to evaluate your progress and set goals for practice. You should also include any useful feedback or pointers from fellow students and instructors. Use this section to identify areas of strength and areas where you need more work.

**Multiple Choice and Essay Questions**

For each chapter, we have provided three multiple choice and two or three essay questions that get at some of the main points of the chapter. The answers to these questions are in Appendix A. If you are not using the textbook, *Learning the Art of Helping,* Third Edition, you may find it difficult to answer the questions in this section, and you may want to skip this part.

**Journal**

Finally, each chapter contains space for your personal journal. You can use the "Journal Starters" provided or refer to others in the textbook. If you wish, you can create your own question or starter to begin your reflection. For each journal entry, write at least two or three paragraphs that encompass both your emotional reaction and your critical thoughts about the material. At times, your instructor may ask you to share the essence of your thinking or read your journal to another student or small group. Reading and reflecting with others is a valuable opportunity to think about your own viewpoint and contrast it with differing ones. You should share only those things that you feel comfortable confiding. The journal is a tool for self-reflection; it is not intended as a means for disclosing your deepest thoughts and feelings to others.

**Appendix A**

Appendix A contains our answers to most of the Written Exercises and all of the Multiple Choice and Essay Questions. The exercises without answers are those that do not have specific right/wrong responses.

**Appendix B**

Appendix B contains four tables for you to refer to as you need them.

Table 1. The Non-judgmental Listening Cycle
    This table shows the basic building block skills and examples of each.

Table 2. Video Evaluation and Student Feedback Form
    This form can be copied and used to evaluate your own session on tape or for an instructor or student to use to give you feedback.

Table 3. Ten Point Rubric for Evaluating Reflecting, Advanced Reflecting, Challenging and
        Goal-setting Skills
    This table can be used to give a global rating of your current progress and indicates some markers of success.

Table 4. Student Interventions During Session & Evaluation of Depth
    This table allows you to write down up to 15 helper interventions and identify the depth of the responses. You can utilize this in your practice sessions or rate your own sessions on tape.

**Give Us Feedback**

We wish you success on your journey to learn the art of helping. If you have ideas about improving this guide, the video segments or the textbook, we would be interested in hearing from you. You may send e-mail to this address: myoung@cfl.rr.com

Mark E. Young
Samantha Chromy

**Video Segments on the Disk that Accompanies *Exercises in the Art of Helping***

| Segment Title | Helper | Client | Starting Time/Clock |
| --- | --- | --- | --- |
| 1. Nonverbal Skills | Chris | Kevin | 00:00 |
| 2. Opening Skills | Mike | Marlene | 03:15 |
| 3. Paraphrasing | Samantha | Stacy | 07:02 |
| 4. Reflecting Feelings I | Chris | Margaret | 10:30 |
| 5. Reflecting Feelings II | Mark | Alisa | 14:00 |
| 6. Reflecting Meaning I | Mark | Santiago | 18:06 |
| 7. Reflecting Meaning II | Dayle | Eve | 24:15 |
| 8. Summarizing | Grant | Liza | 32:01 |
| 9. Nonjudgmental Listening Sequence | Mark | Anna | 36:58 |
| 10. Confrontation I | Mark | NaSundra | 43:18 |
| 11. Confrontation II | Dayle | Catherine | 48:00 |

# Discover the Companion Website Accompanying This Book

## The Prentice Hall Companion Website: A Virtual Learning Environment

Technology is a constantly growing and changing aspect of our field that is creating a need for content and resources. To address this emerging need, Prentice Hall has developed an online learning environment for students and professors alike—Companion Websites—to support our textbooks.

In creating a Companion Website, our goal is to build on and enhance what the textbook already offers. For this reason, the content for each user-friendly website is organized by topic and provides the professor and student with a variety of meaningful resources. Common features of a Companion Website include:

## For the Professor—

Every Companion Website integrates **Syllabus Manager™**, an online syllabus creation and management utility.

- **Syllabus Manager™** provides you, the instructor, with an easy, step-by-step process to create and revise syllabi, with direct links into Companion Website and other online content without having to learn HTML.

- Students may logon to your syllabus during any study session. All they need to know is the web address for the Companion Website and the password you've assigned to your syllabus.

- After you have created a syllabus using **Syllabus Manager™**, students may enter the syllabus for their course section from any point in the Companion Website.

- Clicking on a date, the student is shown the list of activities for the assignment. The activities for each assignment are linked directly to actual content, saving time for students.

- Adding assignments consists of clicking on the desired due date, then filling in the details of the assignment—name of the assignment, instructions, and whether it is a one-time or repeating assignment.

- In addition, links to other activities can be created easily. If the activity is online, a URL can be entered in the space provided, and it will be linked automatically in the final syllabus.

- Your completed syllabus is hosted on our servers, allowing convenient updates from any computer on the Internet. Changes you make to your syllabus are immediately available to your students at their next logon.

**For the Student—**

- **Counseling Topics**—17 core counseling topics represent the diversity and scope of today's counseling field.

- **Annotated Bibliography**—includes seminal foundational works and key current works.

- **Web Destinations**—lists significant and up-to-date practitioner and client sites.

- **Professional Development**—provides helpful information regarding professional organizations and codes of ethics.

- **Electronic Bluebook**—send homework or essays directly to your instructor's email with this paperless form.

- **Message Board**—serves as a virtual bulletin board to post—or respond to—questions or comments to/from a national audience.

- **Chat**—real-time chat with anyone who is using the text anywhere in the country—ideal for discussion and study groups, class projects, etc.

To take advantage of these and other resources, please visit the *Exercises in the Art of Helping,* Third Edition, Companion Website at

**www.prenhall.com/young**

# RESEARCH NAVIGATOR:

# RESEARCH MADE SIMPLE!

**www.ResearchNavigator.com**

Merrill Education is pleased to introduce Research Navigator—a one-stop research solution for students that simplifies and streamlines the entire research process. At www.researchnavigator.com, students will find extensive resources to enhance their understanding of the research process so they can effectively complete research assignments. In addition, Research Navigator has three exclusive databases of credible and reliable source content to help students focus their research efforts and begin the research process.

## How Will Research Navigator Enhance Your Course?

- Extensive content helps students understand the research process, including writing, Internet research, and citing sources.
- Step-by-step tutorial guides students through the entire research process from selecting a topic to revising a rough draft.
- Research Writing in the Disciplines section details the differences in research across disciplines.
- Three exclusive databases—EBSCO's ContentSelect Academic Journal Database, *The New York Times* Search by Subject Archive, and "Best of the Web" Link Library—allow students to easily find journal articles and sources.

## What's the Cost?

A subscription to Research Navigator is $7.50 but is **free** when ordered in conjunction with this textbook. To obtain free passcodes for your students, simply contact your local Merrill/Prentice Hall sales representative, and your representative will send you the Evaluating Online Resource Guide, which contains the code to access Research Navigator as well as tips on how to use Research Navigator and how to evaluate research. To preview the value of this website to your students, please go to www.educatorlearningcenter.com and use the Login Name "Research" and the password "Demo."

# Contents

# Chapter 1
# Helping as a Personal Journey

## Chapter Summary
Individuals who study a completely new area of knowledge go through some predictable stages, as they grow more familiar with the information. Perry described three such stages. The dualistic or "right/wrong" stage is the initial response to a new arena of learning. The multiplistic stage involves recognizing that there may be several "right" ways to respond to a client. Finally, in the relativistic stage, with additional learning and experience, a helper is able to weigh possible responses, depending on the outcome that helper and client are trying to achieve.

Learning the art of helping is a long journey. It takes several years before one can practice independently in the helping profession. Until then, it is helpful to receive supervision as a way of reflecting on the development of one's helping skills. In addition, one can make a commitment to being a "reflective practitioner." A reflective practitioner is one who reviews, evaluates, and plans by thinking and talking about issues as they arise.

Perfectionism can be a roadblock on the journey. Try instead to learn from your mistakes as well as your successes. Find a supportive group of fellow learners, keep a journal, record your training sessions, and use this exercise book to practice and reflect.

## Glossary
*Congruence*: Being genuine in one's interactions with a client. One's thoughts, feelings and actions all correspond.

*Courage to confront*: A willingness to make clients aware of painful issues and risk being disliked.

*Dualistic stage*: This is Perry's first stage, during which learners evaluate their performances as either right or wrong.

*Empathy*: The ability to communicate understanding of a client's feelings and worldview.

*Multiplistic stage*: Perry's stage of development when learners realize that there are several right answers and multiple ways of accomplishing the task.

*Positive regard*: The ability to suspend judgment and accept a person regardless of his or her actions.

*Reflective practitioner*: A reflective practitioner is a professional who makes a commitment to personal awareness by monitoring his or her thinking, automatic reactions, decisions and prejudices by taking time to think back on these reactions and perhaps to record them in a journal or discuss with a supervisor.

*Relativistic stage*: Perry's final stage of cognitive development in which a learner recognizes that some answers are better than others. They can be evaluated on how well the answers fit a particular situation.

**Video Exercises**

Throughout this guide, video exercises appear in this section of each chapter. Frequently, you will be asked to consider how you might respond or to pay attention to certain helper or client reactions. Take a look at the segment entitled "Non-Judgmental Listening Sequence." This is a fairly typical opening sequence as a helper (Mark) tries to learn more about a client (Anna) and her issues. Watch the entire three-minute segment once or twice and then answer the questions below.

**Exercise 1A: Initial Reactions to a Helping Session**

1. How much of the helper's own thoughts, feelings, and ideas came across during this part of the session? If you had been a client would you have wanted the helper to be more involved or less verbal? For what reasons?

_____

_____

2. From your viewpoint, as an observer, did the helper appear to be listening and involved? If so, how did he communicate this?

_____

_____

3. Identify one thing the helper said that seems to encourage the client to tell more of the story.

_____

_____

4. If there is any helper statement you did not like, note it here. What about it made you uncomfortable?

_____

_____

5. Was there any area of the client's story you would like to have known more about? For what reasons?

_____

_____

6. The helper in this video demonstrated a nonjudgmental attitude. How did he avoid taking sides in this conflict between two people?

_____

_____

7. The helper did not give advice to the client. Do you think this would have been helpful? If so, what might you have said?

_____

_____

8. The opinion expressed in this guide is that advice is generally to be avoided. What is your reaction to this guideline with respect to Anna?

_____

_____

9. Discuss your answers with a fellow student. Identify one thing you learned from this sharing of information.

_____

_____

### Written Exercises and Self-Assessment
In the chapters that follow, we have separate sections for Written Exercises and Self-Assessment of your progress in learning the helping skills. Since you are not yet practicing skills, we have combined them here in a self-assessment of your attitudes about helping.

### Assessing Your Helping Characteristics
You may or may not be considering a career in helping. Either way, this exercise can be helpful to gain feedback about your helping characteristics. Listed below are six characteristics that are common to many successful helpers. Ask someone who knows you well to rate you on a 1-10 scale on each of the characteristics. If you are feeling brave, ask two people to make ratings. Ask

those who rate you to be honest so you can receive useful feedback. Try to listen non-defensively if they give you additional verbal feedback. Wait until you are alone to respond to the feedback. React in writing by indicating if you agree or disagree, and when appropriate, give an example to illustrate your point.

<u>Positive View of Humankind.</u> You believe that most people are basically good and striving for self-improvement. You enjoy people and believe they are capable of change.

Rating:

1    2    3    4    5    6    7    8    9    10
*Extremely negative view*                *Extremely Positive view*

Your Reaction:

_____

_____

Is it possible to have a view of people that is too positive or trusting?

_____

_____

<u>Stable and Mentally Healthy.</u> You have good self-esteem and are basically a secure, mentally healthy person. You may not be able to make a completely unbiased self-assessment but friends and family can give you feedback on your coping ability.

Rating:

1    2    3    4    5    6    7    8    9    10
*Unstable and unhealthy*               *Stable and Healthy*

Your reaction:

_____

_____

<u>Good Self-care Skills.</u> You do not become over-involved with those you are helping. You know your limits and are able to set boundaries to protect yourself from burnout.

Rating:

| 1 | 2 | 3 | 4 | 5 | 6 | 7 | 8 | 9 | 10 |
|---|---|---|---|---|---|---|---|---|----|

*Very few self care skills*  
*Rarely take time for self*

*Many skills*  
*Often take time for self-care*

Your reaction:

_____

_____

How might you take better care of yourself?

_____

_____

<u>Intelligent and Psychologically Minded</u>. You are an intellectually curious person who is interested in the psychological worlds of other people. You can appreciate both a scientific and an artistic approach to learning about helping.

Rating:

| 1 | 2 | 3 | 4 | 5 | 6 | 7 | 8 | 9 | 10 |
|---|---|---|---|---|---|---|---|---|----|

*Not very psychologically minded*

*Very psychologically minded*

Your reaction:

_____

_____

Do you think you tend to be more feeling oriented or thinking oriented? Give an example.

_____

_____

<u>Creative</u>. You are a creative person is some aspect of your life. You are not rigid or inflexible in your attitudes. You are not bothered by many prejudices about people, cultures, religions and family customs that differ from your own.

Rating:

1     2     3     4     5     6     7     8     9     10

*Not very creative*                        *Extremely Creative*

Your reaction:

_____

_____

Give an example of your creative side:

_____

_____

<u>Courageous</u>. You have enough courage to examine your own personal problems and seek help and guidance for yourself when you need it. You are willing to admit that you need to change and grow. You are able, for the most part, to deal with the cruelties that other people inflict on each other, without being so disturbed that it disrupts your own life or your ability to help.

Rating:

1     2     3     4     5     6     7     8     9     10

*Not very self aware*                  *Very self aware*

*Avoid painful issues*                 *Willing to look at painful issues*

Your reaction:

_____

_____

Give an example:

_____

_____

**Multiple Choice and Short Essay Questions**

Multiple choice and essay questions are provided so that you can test your understanding of the material presented in the textbook, Learning the Art of Helping. They may help you prepare for tests given by your instructor. The answers to the multiple choice questions are provided in the Appendix. If you are not using the textbook with this CD and study guide, it may not be possible to answer all of the questions.

1. According to Perry, which of the three stages is characterized by "right/wrong" thinking?
   a. dualistic
   b. multiplistic
   c. ritualistic
   d. relativistic

2. A journeyman is:
   a. a master practitioner
   b. a layperson
   c. a person who can do a day's labor unsupervised
   d. an expert

3. Congruence means:
   a. being consistently genuine in thought, word and deed
   b. being ethical
   c. being sympathetic and empathic
   d. an attitude of genuine acceptance

4. Compare and contrast the stages of development described by Perry with the skilled trades notion of expertise. In the trades, one moves from a novice to a journeyman, to an expert and finally to a master. Both are looking at the development of knowledge and skills but there are distinct differences. Which do you think is most applicable to learning the art of helping?

5. Besides learning skills, this chapter suggests that a helper must have or develop specific attitudes. What attitudes are recommended? Does this mean that a helper without these attitudes is handicapped? Does this mean that all helpers must come from a specific mold?

**Journal**

A journal is a personal space for reflection about what you are learning in this course and a way of integrating this new knowledge with what you already know. In this guide we have left a space for you to write with pencil or pen. You can instead use a computer, purchase a blank book or develop a three-ring binder to construct a journal that allows you to add other information such as important articles, poems, pictures, etc. Bring your reflections to class or share them privately with your instructor. Because this class invites so much personal growth, your instructor may ask you to journal several times during the semester. Try to be as honest as you can, but think about what you share too, not only in a journal but what you confide in your classmates. It may be possible to share too much about a particular topic and overwhelm others. Whether you are asked to share some of your journal or not, approach it with complete honesty and edit it later.

Choose one of the suggestions below and allow yourself to express your own ideas, feelings and personal reflections in the space provided.

1. Think about a time when you think that you really helped someone. What did you do and say that seemed to have been especially helpful? Contrast this, if you can, with another time when you tried to help but you were not as successful. What was different about the two situations?

2. Think about your previous relationships with significant others in your life. What are the best and worst parts of your personality? How might these show up in your relationships with clients?

3. Think about times in your life when you have not been as successful as you wanted to be. How did you react? What helped you overcome the problem? How can you best deal with setbacks in your basic helping skills training? What feelings do you have as you start this process?

# Chapter 2
# The Nuts and Bolts of Helping

**Chapter Summary**

One can help as a professional or as a non-professional. Friends take turns in helping each other at different stages of life. Friendship has other goals besides helping, such as mutual affection and play. Professional helping, by contrast, is a contractual relationship in which a helper and a client agree on goals and a form of payment for the helper. Professional helping can be divided into interviewing, counseling, and psychotherapy, which overlap considerably.

Beginning helpers usually have a number of unrealistic expectations about the process of helping others. For the most part these are perfectionistic ideas that suggest we should be able to help all people at all times. Each helper has unique personality traits, gifts and skills to bring to the helping relationship. Similarly, each client is unique and will differ in his or her response to the helper, and in how motivated he or she is to make changes.

The notion of therapeutic or common curative factors is introduced in this chapter. These therapeutic factors are ways of understanding and organizing helping techniques in terms of an underlying therapeutic force that is presumed to account for their effectiveness. These factors are: 1) the therapeutic relationship; 2) enhancing efficacy and self-esteem; 3) practicing new behaviors; 4) lowering and raising emotional arousal; 5) activating expectations, motivation and hope; and 6) new learning experiences. Under each factor you will learn several techniques. For example, when a client is having trouble with self-esteem, you will be familiar with a number of treatment methods for this problem area.

The helping relationship is described as proceeding through several stages. The following five-stage model gives you an idea of how a typical helping relationship may progress over time. At each stage, the helper and client each have a role in moving the process forward. In the first stage, Relationship Building, the helper provides a therapeutic relationship where the client feels safe to disclose important issues. The second stage, Assessment, is when the helper invites the client to provide information, and focuses on assessment. In the third stage, Goal Setting, the helper and client develop plans for treatment by narrowing down the problems to be addressed and by setting goals. In the fourth stage, Intervention and Action, the helper delivers interventions and uses techniques to help the client achieve his or her goals. Also during this stage, the client takes action and moves toward achieving the agreed upon goals. Finally, in the fifth stage, Outcome Evaluation and Termination, the helper and client evaluate their progress and reflect on the progress made. Together they determine how helping should proceed or whether it should end. The nuts and bolts of helping involve learning the definitions and stages of the helping relationship as a preparation for the upcoming chapters, focused primarily on skills.

**Glossary**

*Helping*: Helping is broadest possible description of the relationship between any two people where one gives and the other receives assistance. This may occur within or outside of a professional environment.

*Professional helping*: The term describes a contractual relationship between a helper and client who agree on compensation for the helper and goals for the client.

*Interviewing*: Interviewing is not necessarily helping, and the interviewee is not necessarily a client of the interviewer. The client may be an entity other than the person being interviewed, such as an agency, corporation, or school. The purpose may not be to help the interviewee but to make a decision about treatment, hiring, or placement.

*Counseling*: The goals for counseling are usually to help clients overcome normal developmental hurdles. Counseling goals are growth oriented and emphasize the therapeutic relationship as a major factor. The distinction between counseling and psychotherapy, in practice, is difficult to draw since counseling may also involve helping people with mental disorders.

*Psychotherapy*: Compared to counseling, psychotherapy is helping that relies on accurate diagnosis, emphasizes pathology, and is more concerned with treating mental disorders.

*Therapeutic factors*: These are the common curative forces that underlie the helping techniques. In this book, we recognize six therapeutic factors.

*Building blocks*: The therapeutic building blocks are the basic or elementary skills that one learns in the beginning to build more complex techniques. There are 22 therapeutic building blocks described in this book.

**Written Exercises**
**Exercise 2A: Reasonable and Unreasonable Ideas about Learning the Art of Helping**

When you are practicing, or working with actual clients, you might find you have negative thoughts that can undermine your self-confidence. Discouragement can affect your performance. Listed below are some of the unrealistic ideas about helping that might come to mind. See if you can argue with these ideas by writing down a more reasonable expectation after each unreasonable one. When these ideas spring up during training, refer back to this exercise and try substituting the more reasonable thoughts before the unreasonable one affects your confidence.

1.  Unreasonable: "I am not learning these skills as quickly as I want to. I am not the best in the class, therefore I am terrible."

    More Reasonable Thought to Substitute:

    _____
    _____
    _____

2.  Unreasonable: "I read the book and practiced the skill twice but I can't do it. Therefore, I will never learn it."

    More Reasonable Thought to Substitute:

    _____
    _____
    _____

3. Unreasonable: "I am listening to the client but we have not solved all of the client's problems. Listening is a waste of time."

   More Reasonable Thought to Substitute:

   _____

   _____

   _____

4. Unreasonable: "I don't really like this client or relate to his problems. I should like every client."

   More Reasonable Thought to Substitute:

   _____

   _____

   _____

5. Unreasonable: "Sometimes I can perform a skill well and other times I seem unable to. I have not really learned anything because I only perform the skill occasionally."

   More Reasonable Thought to Substitute:

   _____

   _____

   _____

Based on your previous experience, which of these is most likely to arise in your mind when you are not successful?

   _____

   _____

   _____

## Self-Assessment
### Efficacy and Self-Esteem

One of the therapeutic factors involves enhancing client efficacy and self-esteem. Efficacy is the expectation that you can do something well. For example, you may be confident about your ability to sit down at a keyboard and type. Turn your attention to the interpersonal sphere of functioning. You already possess many useful skills. Think about what you are good at when it comes to dealing with other people. While you are learning new skills, it is important to remember your present strengths and find a way to incorporate them with your new helping skills. How do you rate yourself on the following skills? I am confident that I can:

1. Talk to people about serious and painful subjects without being overwhelmed:

| 1 | 2 | 3 | 4 | 5 | 6 | 7 | 8 | 9 | 10 |

*Not at all confident*                              *Very confident*

2. Chat, make small talk, and keep a conversation going:

| 1 | 2 | 3 | 4 | 5 | 6 | 7 | 8 | 9 | 10 |
|---|---|---|---|---|---|---|---|---|---|

*Not at all confident*                                                    *Very confident*

3. Make people feel comfortable:

| 1 | 2 | 3 | 4 | 5 | 6 | 7 | 8 | 9 | 10 |
|---|---|---|---|---|---|---|---|---|---|

*Not at all confident*                                                    *Very confident*

4. Allow other people to cry or express emotions:

| 1 | 2 | 3 | 4 | 5 | 6 | 7 | 8 | 9 | 10 |
|---|---|---|---|---|---|---|---|---|---|

*Not at all confident*                                                    *Very confident*

5. Help people figure out answers to their problems:

| 1 | 2 | 3 | 4 | 5 | 6 | 7 | 8 | 9 | 10 |
|---|---|---|---|---|---|---|---|---|---|

*Not at all confident*                                                    *Very confident*

6. Make people think by posing challenging questions:

| 1 | 2 | 3 | 4 | 5 | 6 | 7 | 8 | 9 | 10 |
|---|---|---|---|---|---|---|---|---|---|

*Not at all confident*                                                    *Very confident*

7. Talk about myself, my feelings and ideas:

| 1 | 2 | 3 | 4 | 5 | 6 | 7 | 8 | 9 | 10 |
|---|---|---|---|---|---|---|---|---|---|

*Not at all confident*                                                    *Very confident*

8. Challenge people when they are not being honest with themselves:

| 1 | 2 | 3 | 4 | 5 | 6 | 7 | 8 | 9 | 10 |
|---|---|---|---|---|---|---|---|---|---|

*Not at all confident*                                                    *Very confident*

9. Describe any other skill that you have that you might be able to transfer to the helping relationship:

_____

_____

10. Review the skills listed above and select two that you feel fairly confident about. Think about how you might go overboard in using that skill. What might happen if the skill was used incorrectly?

_____

_____

_____

_____

**Multiple Choice and Short Essay Questions**

1. Which of these is <u>not</u> one of the common curative or therapeutic factors?
   a. practicing new behaviors
   b. assertiveness
   c. enhancing efficacy and self-esteem
   d. new learning experiences

2. In which stage of helping do the helper and client formally consider whether to continue the relationship?
   a. assessment and giving information
   b. treatment planning and goal-setting
   c. evaluation and reflection
   d. intervention and action

3. Interviewing is different than other aspects of helping because:
   a. the interviewee may not be helped by the interview.
   b. interviewing is stressful.
   c. interviewing involves only questions.
   d. interviewing may be done in groups.

4. List and describe each of the five stages of the helping relationship.

5. Of the six therapeutic factors described here, which do you feel may be the most important in the beginning and which may be the most important to emphasize later in the helping process? Give a rationale for your choice.

**Journal**

1. Think about helping someone who is very different from you. Perhaps someone who is much older or someone who is combating a drug addiction. How would you feel about working with a person like that? What about one who is very depressed or who has a serious mental disorder? What sort of preparation and what sort of support would you want to have if you daily faced such issues?

2. Think about some key friendships in your life. What is it that has made them so important for you? Compare you feelings of closeness in your friendship with your feelings about favorite teachers you have known. For a relationship to be productive, do you think that emotional closeness and liking are essential?

3. Rescuing is sometimes defined as doing more than 50% of the work in a helping relationship. Have you ever helped someone who did not put in much effort to help themselves? How did you end up feeling? As you think about that, how do you think this feeling on your part affected your relationship? Suppose your job was to work with court-ordered individuals, how would you like helping people who say they don't want help?

# Chapter 3
# The Therapeutic Relationship

**Chapter Summary**

A strong alliance between helper and client is vital to the success of the helping enterprise. A good working relationship is the best predictor of client goal attainment. The helping relationship differs from social relationships. A therapeutic relationship focuses on the client's issues and there is a sense of teamwork toward mutually agreed upon goals. The relationship is contractual, with understandings about confidentiality and compensation for services.

Helpers can enhance the quality of the therapeutic relationship through non-verbal skills including physical closeness, posture, and warmth. In addition, helpers try to increase their own cultural awareness, expertness and credibility to strengthen the bond with a client. Similarly, several factors may strain the therapeutic relationship. These include inappropriate self-disclosure by the helper, distractions, mismatches between client and helper, and transference and counter-transference. In addition, the relationship can falter when the helper makes therapeutic faux pas such as being punitive, using psychobabble, advancing premature interpretations, and probing issues that the client strongly resists. Transference and countertransference issues may also create problems for helpers when clients see them unrealistically or when they allow personal feelings to intrude into the therapeutic relationship.

**Glossary**

*Countertransference*: This refers to the helper's reactions to a client. These originate in past relationships or personal issues, and are transferred to the client or on to the helping relationship. For example, the helper responds very passively toward the client, because he or she has had difficulty handling domineering people in an assertive manner.

*Credibility*: The client's perception that their helper is a competent professional with the ability and qualifications to help them. Credibility enhances the therapeutic relationship.

*Empathy*: The ability to grasp the facts, feelings, and significance of another's story and convey this understanding to them. It is the ability to "feel oneself into" another's experience.

*Schmoozing*: The interactions between helper and client that are social in nature and not directly related to the client's problems. Examples include discussing the weather or a client's hobby.

*Therapeutic faux pas*: Helper responses that may weaken or disrupt the helping relationship. For example, criticizing the client is generally considered inappropriate.

*Transference*: Client feelings from past relationships or personal issues that are carried over to the helper or helping relationship. For example, the client feels anger towards a male helper due to past abusive experiences with men.

**Video Exercises**

**Exercise 3A: Analyzing the Therapeutic Relationship**

1. Review the video segment *Opening Skills* (04:04 to 06:52). In this segment Mike (the helper) is able to create an atmosphere of warmth when talking with Marlene (client). Describe the helper's non-verbal behaviors that help create warmth in this session.

_____

_____

2. Review video segment *Reflecting Feelings II* (14:03-17:54) and watch for evidence of empathy by the helper (see definition in Glossary). Write down three statements by Mark (the helper) that communicate understanding of Lisa's (the client) situation.

   a. _____

   b. _____

   c. _____

3. Write down Lisa's responses to Mark's three statements that you identified above.

   a. _____

   b. _____

   c. _____

   What effect did these statements have on Lisa?

   _____

   _____

4. Review video segment *Paraphrasing* (07:39 to 10:28), and consider the statement, "empathy is not merely agreeing with the client." Samantha (the helper) appears to empathize with Stacey (the client) without agreeing with her statements that her boyfriend "is the problem." What words did Samantha use to communicate this neutral stance?

   _____

   _____

_____

_____

5. At 8:45 (*Paraphrasing*), Stacey implies that the helper has an easy job just like the client's boyfriend. If this were a social situation, how might you respond to this challenge? If you were Samantha, how would you have responded to this innuendo?

_____

_____

_____

_____

6. Notice the décor of the office shown on the video. What words would you use to describe it? Do you consider this to be a facilitative office environment? What do you like or dislike about it?

_____

_____

_____

_____

**Written Exercises**

**Exercise 3B:  Identifying Appropriate Helper Self-Disclosure**

Below are some examples of inappropriate helper self-disclosure. In the space provided, record a more appropriate helper disclosure. The first situation is completed as an example.

1.  Situation: The client feels anger toward her boss because she believes he is mistreating her.

Inappropriate helper self-disclosure:

"I remember I once was so mad at my boss that I thought about letting the air out of her tires."

Appropriate helper self-disclosure:

"I've had challenges with bosses. When things are not going well at work, it seems to affect the rest of your life, too."

Now, you try it.

2. Situation: The client is dealing with grief from the death of a spouse.

Inappropriate helper self-disclosure: "My grandmother died about two years ago, I found I got over it reasonably quickly."

Appropriate helper self-disclosure:

_____

_____

3. Situation: The client has problems with excessive alcohol use.

Inappropriate helper self-disclosure: "I am a recovering alcoholic. I used to drink a bottle of whiskey a day; I was often drunk at work."

Appropriate helper self-disclosure:

_____

_____

4. Situation: The client is suffering with depression.

Inappropriate helper self-disclosure: "I am lucky, I've never been depressed."

Appropriate helper self-disclosure:

_____

_____

5. Situation: The client is hoping to be accepted into graduate school.

Inappropriate helper self-disclosure: "Exams can be so difficult; I failed to pass an important entrance exam once."

Appropriate helper self-disclosure:

_____

_____

**Exercise 3C: Roadblocks Exercise**

A roadblock is a response by the helper that cuts off communication. Read the client situations below each roadblock. First create a "roadblock response," and then follow this with an appropriate helping response that encourages the client to open up. As an example, the first roadblock is filled out for you. Note that the Roadblock Response we have supplied exemplifies Ordering, Directing, or Commanding, a statement that disrupts helper/client communication. When it comes to creating a more appropriate helper response, don't worry too much about creating the perfect intervention. The aim of the exercise is to recognize that there are alternatives to these common obstacles.

1. Ordering, Directing, Commanding.

Client: "I am thinking of leaving my wife."

Roadblock Response:

"You'd better get to marriage counseling right away."

Appropriate helper response:

"Sounds like you have been having serious trouble with your relationship. Can you tell me more about it?"

Now, it's your turn.

2. Moralizing, Preaching, Imploring.

Client: "I am confused about whether or not to stop drinking alcohol, it relaxes me after work."

Roadblock Response:

_____

_____

_____

Appropriate helper response:

_____

_____

_____

3.  Advising, Giving Suggestions, or Solutions.

Client: "I want to lose weight, I'm just too fat."
Roadblock Response:

_____

_____

_____

Appropriate helper response:

_____

_____

_____

4.  Judging, Criticizing, Disagreeing, Blaming.

Client: "I decided not to go to work today. I spent all morning in bed reading magazines."

Roadblock Response:

_____

_____

_____

Appropriate helper response:

_____

_____

_____

5.  Interpreting, Analyzing, Diagnosing.

Client: "My son Bobby took some money from my purse the other day. He's done it before, but I don't say anything as I might hurt his feelings."

Roadblock Response:

_____

_____

_____

Appropriate helper response:

_____

_____

_____


6.  Reassuring, Sympathizing, Consoling, Supporting.

Client: "She left me again last night after a big fight. I think she is staying at her lover's house."

Roadblock Response:

_____

_____

_____

Appropriate helper response:

_____

_____

_____


7.  Probing, Questioning, Interrogating.

Client: "This is my third speeding ticket this month."

Roadblock Response:

_____

_____

_____

Appropriate helper response:

_____

_____

_____


8.  Distracting, Diverting, Kidding.

Client: "I don't know if things will ever improve for me."

Roadblock Response:

_____

_____

_____

Appropriate helper response:

_____

_____

_____

**Multiple Choice and Essay Questions**

1.  Which of the following is <u>not</u> an example of counter-transference?
    a.  Sexual attraction toward the client.
    b.  Feeling intimidated by a client.
    c.  Listening attentively to the client's story.
    d.  Telling the client a personal problem.

2.  Which of the following is <u>not</u> considered a therapeutic faux pas or roadblock?
    a.  Empathizing.
    b.  Advice-giving.
    c.  Consoling.
    d.  Using psychological jargon.

3.  Which of the following statements is most accurate?
    a.  Helpers should exaggerate their credentials to enhance their credibility.
    b.  A strong client/helper alliance is a good predictor of positive therapeutic outcome.
    c.  A client-helper relationship is the same as a good friendship.
    d.  Giving clear advice enhances the therapeutic relationship.

4.  Briefly describe four differences between the helper/client relationship and a social relationship.

5. How can a helper increase credibility with a client? What would you consider to be ethical and what would be unethical?

## Journal

Choose one of the suggestions below and allow yourself to express your own ideas, feelings, and personal reflections in the space provided.

1. Think for a moment about an important friendship in your life. Reflect on the ups and downs in the relationship and the stages that the relationship has gone through. What is it that makes this relationship special?

2. Consider the topic of anger in your journal. Look back over the past few months and think about times that anger has surfaced in your life. Reflect now about the ways that anger was expressed in your family. Have there been times when anger has caused significant problems in relationships? Has suppressing your needs and trying to be a "nice person" always been helpful? How do you think you might deal with a client's anger as a helper? What about your own feelings of anger when they arise in the helping session?

3. Recall a relationship, past or present, where the other person was significantly different from you, either in age, culture, or ethnicity. Discuss the experience. Was the development of the relationship more challenging than with someone more similar to you? In what ways? How did your differences enhance or deter from the relationship? How did overcome any obstacles to communication? What did you learn from the experience?

# Chapter 4
# Helping Someone Who Is Different

## Chapter Summary

The major point of Chapter 4 is that differences can affect the therapeutic alliance. There are an infinite number of differences between people including personality, race, gender, culture, ethnicity, socioeconomic status and so on. Stage of life differences can create a gulf between clients who want older helpers or who prefer someone nearer their own age. Much has been described in the literature about trying to match helpers and clients but, in reality, most settings do not allow for this.

In this chapter, we looked at two differences in more detail: gender and culture. Both affect us whether we know it to or not. We discussed the knowledge, skills, and attitudes needed to establish a relationship with someone who is different in one of these two ways. Culture is a pervasive force that colors our worldview and attitudes. The helper must expose himself or herself to a wide variety of cultural experiences to have a broad understanding of how cultures see things differently. The example of internal/external locus of control is described in this chapter as one way that we can conceptualize the variety of attitudes that are affected by our background. It is asserted that a helper must have an attitude of openness that allows him or her to recognize the different forces that have shaped the lives of their clients. Similarly, the skills that a culturally competent helper will have include an understanding that not all techniques will be effective when there are cultural barriers.

Gender differences may appear to be less difficult to deal with; however, the volumes written about gender and communication have made us aware that even in work and social settings, gender training can affect our ability to get along with others. In the helping relationship, the helper needs to have knowledge of the differences in communication. Helpers must also be aware of attitudes caused by their own gender training such as expecting men to be strong or women to be accommodating can influence the session and may work against the therapeutic goals. The helper must develop skills of self-reflection through supervision, and be able to assess these issues at the beginning of the relationship.

In this chapter, the author is making a case for a "client centered eclecticism" that asks the helper to design the therapeutic interventions around the needs of the client. By tailoring the treatment to the client, we may be going against traditional theoretical orientations that prescribe based on diagnosis or because the theory utilizes only specific techniques.

## Glossary

*Sex*: Refers to basic physiological differences between men and women.

*Gender*: Refers to the roles that each sex is taught.

*Acculturated*: The degree to which one has adopted the worldview and participates in prescribed activities of a particular cultural group.

*Internal/External Locus of Control*: Rotter's traditional distinction between those who believe that their fate is self controlled or controlled by the environment.

*Culturally Competent*: This refers to a helper who has the knowledge, skills, and attitudes to work with those that are culturally different.

*Worldview*: The sum total of an individual's beliefs about self, others, and the world. The worldview is significantly influenced by an individual's experiences and culture.

*Culturally Encapsulated*: This refers to an individual who is not culturally competent and who is unable to transcend the boundaries of his or her own cultural experiences.

*Ascribed/Achieved Credibility*: In this context, credibility means being perceived by clients as a potential helper. Cultures differ in those who are ascribed credibility. For example, being a teacher or being older might give one credibility automatically. Another way to achieve credibility is by helping a client create a significant change.

*Similar-to-me Effect*: This is a common error or distortion identified by social psychologists that occurs when we show preference for someone who is like us (was a member of our sorority, came from the same state, is of the same racial background). This effect is a form of encapsulation.

*Prescriptive Eclecticism*: A term used to describe the approach of tailoring the treatment to the client. This approach is considered by the author to be a more culturally appropriate method for planning treatment rather than adhering to a single theoretical viewpoint.

**Written Exercises**
**Exercise 4A: Self-Assessment: Are you a Culturally Competent Helper?**

No helper can expect to have the knowledge, skills and attitudes necessary to deal with all kinds of clients. As you proceed on your journey, you will run into a variety of situations that may cause you discomfort or confusion. Read the descriptions below and check those that might currently be a challenge for you to accept:

_____ Your client does not speak English very well, and wishes to stay outside of the mainstream culture –not interacting or really accepting the dominant culture.

_____ Your client is a Muslim. She believes that the answers to life's problems can be found in the teachings of Islam.

_____ Your client is a non-traditional male who stays home with the children and has little interest in career.

_____ Your client is GLBT (Gay, Lesbian, Bisexual, or Transgendered). He or she is not interested in changing this.

_____ Your client views his or her grandparents as wise and often defers important decisions to them.

_____ Your client has four children from different fathers and has never been married. The client considers her family structure to include her children and her mother.

_____ Your client has culturally different ideas about child discipline. You find them excessively harsh.

_____ Your client does not trust Western medicine and prefers traditional medical procedures from India.

_____ Your client's non-verbals seem to suggest that she is cold and unresponsive. You are not certain.

What sort of training would help you develop the knowledge, skills and attitudes you need to deal with the situations you have identified?

_____

_____

_____

_____

## Multiple Choice and Essay Questions

1. The general approach of using methods and techniques that take into account the client's unique background is called:
   a. Cultural competency
   b. Prescriptive eclecticism
   c. Cultural encapsulation
   d. Uniqueness training

2. *Ascribed credibility* refers to:
   a. The tendency to approach all clients the same
   b. Using only empirically validated methods in helping
   c. The degree of potency granted by the culture to a helper based on age, profession etc.
   d. Techniques that will be rejected by a culture because they are not believable

3. If you are a man counseling a woman, one of the issues you may have to deal with is:
   a. You are treating the client as being fragile or ineffective
   b. You are leading and expecting the client to follow
   c. The client is dealing with role strain and role conflict
   d. All of the above

4. The essence of this chapter is that differences can cause a rift in the therapeutic relationship and that it is up to the helper to be aware and accepting of differences. What can a helper do when he or she is faced with someone from a vastly different culture or socioeconomic background? What basic steps must the helper take?

5. A great deal of the training for helpers in dealing with different cultures is based on gaining knowledge about stereotypical ways that members of a culture respond interpersonally or to the helping process; i.e., Latinos generally... For the most part, African Americans... This may be unavoidable because writers are trying to inform the reader about the average person in the culture. Why is it not safe to rely entirely on these generalizations? How might a helper deal most effectively with these situations?

**Journal**

1. Have you ever experienced "culture shock," the feeling that you were isolated and confused in a different country or culture? If so, write about this experience. Do you think that everyone who has grown up in a different culture experiences this when they immigrate? How do people respond to these feelings? What do they do? How can a helper assist someone with culture shock?

2. Let us suppose that a client met you and then immediately asked for a different helper because you were not of the same nationality, culture, age, sex, or for some other reason related to outer differences. How would you react? What issues would it raise for you?

# Chapter 5
# Invitational Skills

## Chapter Summary
Invitational skills are the elementary listening skills that a helper uses to indicate a willingness to hear the client's story. Invitational skills include two categories of facilitative behaviors: nonverbal skills and opening skills. The helper uses body language and nonverbal skills to create the optimal setting for the client to feel comfortable. Invitational skills include appropriate eye contact, body position, attentive silence, gestures, facial expressions, voice tone, physical distance, and even physical touch. Opening skills, on the other hand, are the verbal messages sent by the helper to facilitate client disclosure. These include minimal encouragers, door openers, open questions, and closed questions. When used appropriately, invitational skills convey warmth, understanding, and attention, and create a safe environment for the client to explore even deep, painful material.

## Glossary
*Facilitative body position*: A helper's body posture is facilitative when it communicates interest, relaxation, and openness. It encourages the client's communication and comfort. It is also referred to as a "posture of involvement".

*Gestures*: Gestures are facial expressions and hand and body movements when they are used as communication. Gestures can facilitate client communication or become distractions for the client.

*Attentive silence*: These are small periods of silence when the helper remains present and attentive to the client. These periods of silence allow time for client and helper contemplation, and may encourage further disclosure from the client.

*Minimal encouragers*: Minimal encouragers are short supportive statements that indicate that the helper is paying attention and understands the client. They are useful to nudge the client to continue yet they do no intrude and distract. Examples include "Okay." and "I'm with you."

*Door openers*: Door openers are "non-coercive invitations to talk." They are requests for the client to continue or expand. Examples include, "Help me understand more about that." and "Go on."

*Closed Questions*: These questions require short, factual responses or yes/no responses. Examples include, "How long were you married?" and "Are you angry?" Closed questions are not the most effective invitational skills but are important for eliciting key pieces of information.

*Open questions*: Open questions direct the client to talk about a particular subject, but are less demanding in comparison to closed questions. While they may suggest an area for exploration, they give the client a wider range of possible responses. Because of this, they encourage the client to open up rather than supply a single piece of data. "Can you tell me about your marriage?" is an example of an open question.

**Video Exercises**

**Exercise 5A: Focusing on Body Language**

Watch the video segment titled *Nonverbal Skills* showing Chris, a helper, and Kevin, her client. Watch the entire segment first, and then answer the questions below.

1. Would you describe Chris's body posture as attentive and open? If so, what gives you this impression?

_____

_____

_____

2. At 2:29 the helper touches the client's arm. Would you, as a helper, have touched the client at this point? Why or Why not? How did the client react?

_____

_____

_____

3. Look through this segment and see if you can find instances where the helper changed her voice to match the client's tone.

_____

_____

_____

4. Would you characterize Chris's manner as warm? If so, what does she do to communicate this?

_____

_____

_____

5. See if you can identify any point where Chris uses attentive silence.

_____

_____

_____

6. What effect does this have on Kevin?

_____

_____

_____

**Written Exercises**
**Exercise 5B: Labeling Opening Skills**
Read the following excerpt from a counseling session between a helper, Montserrat, and her new client, Kathy. Classify each of the following helper responses as a door opener, minimal encourager, open question or closed question.

<u>Skill Used</u>

Montserrat: Could you share with me a little about what prompted you to schedule this appointment.    1._____

Kathy: Well, my husband has been on the computer every evening for the last six months or so, sometimes until 1:00 A. M.

Montserrat: Okay.    2._____

Kathy: I don't know what to do!

Montserrat: Tell me some more about it.    3._____

Kathy: Well, I discovered that my husband has been downloading inappropriate material from the internet.

Montserrat: When you say "inappropriate" do you mean pornographic?    4._____

Kathy: Yes.

Montserrat: It sounds like this bothers you…    5._____

Kathy: Bothers me? I am totally devastated!

Montserrat: Go on…    6._____

Kathy: I'm humiliated!

Montserrat: How did you find out about his activities?    7._____

| Kathy: | I was going through the old e-mail files and I saw all these advertisements from web sites he has visited. | |
|---|---|---|
| Montserrat: | Have you confronted him with what you discovered? | 8._____ |
| Kathy: | No, I just found out about it an hour or two ago. He's not home from work yet. | |
| Montserrat: | Can you tell me a little about things have been going in your relationship? | 9._____ |

**Exercise 5C: More Practice in Classifying Helper Opening Skills**

As in the last exercise, read the following excerpt from a counseling session between a helper, Mrs. Henderson, and her new student, Maryann. Classify each of the following helper responses as a door opener, minimal encourager, open question or closed question.

<u>Skill Used</u>

| Mrs. Henderson: | It looks like you've been crying, Maryann | 1._____ |
|---|---|---|
| Maryann: | Yes, that is why I came to see you. | |
| Mrs. Henderson: | Can you tell me what's upsetting you? | 2._____ |
| Maryann: | Everything! I hate this school! | |
| Mrs. Henderson: | Go on. | 3._____ |
| Maryann: | I hate the other kids, and I hate my teacher. | |
| Mrs. Henderson: | Tell me some more about what has been happening. | 4._____ |
| Maryann: | Well, ever since I moved here, Joe and Maggie have been calling me names. | |
| Mrs. Henderson: | And how long ago was that? | 5._____ |
| Maryann: | About half a year now. | |
| Mrs. Henderson: | What kind of things are they saying? | 6._____ |

| Maryann: | That I'm fat and ugly. Someone called me stupid today. | |
|---|---|---|
| Mrs. Henderson: | Okay, go on. | 7._____ |
| Maryann: | It happens a lot. It's not fair. | |
| Mrs. Henderson: | What has it been like – having to deal with this? | 8._____ |
| Maryann: | Horrible! I feel like I want to go back to my old school in Ohio. I had lots of friends there. | |

Respond to Maryann's last statement with an opening skill:

_____

_____

_____

How would you classify it?                                    9._____

### Exercise 5D: Responding Using Opening Skills

Following the client statements below are blanks for an appropriate helper response. Write in an opening skill of the type indicated to the right of the blank.

| Robert (client): | Now that I talk about it, it sounds like such a silly problem, but I can't seem to get past it. | |
|---|---|---|
| Marty (helper): | _____ | (Door Opener) |
| | _____ | |
| Robert: | Simply put, I can't stand my father in law. | |
| Marty: | _____ | (Minimal Encourager) |
| Robert: | I don't think he has ever approved of me. He thinks I'm not good enough for his daughter and that I don't have a good enough job or income. It makes me so mad. | |

Marty: _____ (Open question)

_____

Robert: Well, he pretty much ignores me on social occasions, except the odd comment about my job like "still an assistant, Robert?"

Marty: _____ (Minimal Encourager)

Robert: And he talks to my wife about how financially successful other family members are. Basically, he compares me to the rich ones.

Marty: _____ (Open question)

_____

Robert: It makes me feel lousy about myself, like he is right, that I am no good. I hate feeling that way.

Marty: _____ (Door Opener)

_____

## Exercise 5E: More Practice Using Opening Skills

Read the following client statements. Insert an appropriate helper response, of the type indicated to the right. Jack is the client and Mr. Green is the helper.

Jack (client): Miss Hightower said I had to come and see you.

Mr. Green (helper): _____ (Door Opener)

_____

Jack: I don't know – something to do with Peter Galla and me.

Mr. Green: _____ (Minimal Encourager)

Jack:    Well, we got in a bit of a fight. But he told
         Miss Hightower it was all my fault and that
         I started it. That wasn't how it happened.

Mr. Green:    _____    (Open question)

              _____

Jack:    I was doing my work, and trying to keep out
         of everyone's way. I've been trying to stay
         out of trouble, since there were those other
         fights last semester. But he kept calling my
         girlfriend names. I told him to stop, but he
         wouldn't.

Mr. Green:    _____    (Door Opener)

              _____

Jack:    Then I just swung at him. Before I knew it
         we were on the floor fighting. I think a chair
         got broken.

Mr. Green:    _____    (Closed question)

              _____

## Self-Assessment

Conduct a practice session with two fellow students, one will be the "client" and the other will be an observer. Then fill out the feedback forms below. The topic need not involve a significant issue since opening and nonverbal skills can be used in nearly all situations.

To the Observer:
Please respond as honestly as possible to the following statements using the 5-point scale below:

| 1 | 2 | 3 | 4 | 5 |
|---|---|---|---|---|
| Strongly Disagree | Disagree | Neutral | Agree | Strongly Agree |

Response

1.  The helper's level of eye contact seemed comfortable and appropriate.    _____

2.  The helper's body position conveyed interest and attention.    _____

3. The helper allowed some periods of silence during the session. _____

4. The helper's voice tone was calm and concerned. _____

5. The physical distance between the helper and client seemed comfortable. _____

6. The helper's body language was relaxed and comfortable. _____

7. The client talked more than the helper. _____

8. The helper asked only a few closed questions. _____

9. The helper used more open questions than closed questions. _____

Please identify one or two things the helper did well in the session

1. _____

2. _____

Please identify one or two things the helper can do to further improve his or her skills.

1. _____

2. _____

To the Helper:

Based on the feedback you received, identify one or two things you hope to work on in upcoming practice sessions.

1. _____

2. _____

**Multiple Choice and Short Essay Questions**

1. Which of the following responses below is the best example of an open question?
   a. How many times per week do you play tennis?
   b. Are you feeling sad?
   c. How did you get through that experience?
   d. Tell me some more about your childhood.

2. Which of the following statements is <u>most</u> accurate?
   a. A helper should sit behind a desk as this creates an air of professionalism.
   b. Hugging a client creates a strong bond in the early stages of the helping relationship.
   c. Closed questions should be used primarily to gain important facts and information.
   d. In order to make the client feel relaxed, it is recommended that the helper lean back in the chair and even put his or her feet on the desk.

3. Nonverbal skills are (select the best response):
   a. silence
   b. body language
   c. sign language
   d. not used in helping

4. Describe the recommended use of eye contact by a helper, and any cultural differences that should be considered.

5. Describe the main differences between open and closed questions. When would you use each type of question?

**Journal**

Select one of the "starters" below to begin your journal for this chapter. Remember that starters are designed to warm you up to these issues. You may take them in whatever direction you like. You need not answer every question if they distract you from an important thought or stop the flow of ideas.

1. Consider a time in your life when you shared the details of a painful problem with a friend or helper. Was it helpful? If so, how did the person respond to you that allowed the sharing to be a positive experience? If it was not helpful, what conclusions have you drawn from that experience?

2. Consider your views on the role of physical touch in the helping relationship. Then reflect on the culture and family in which you were raised. At what times was physical affection shown? How frequent was touch among family members? Was physical affection between non-family members, such as friends, considered appropriate? Reflect on the ways family and cultural norms affected these views.

3. Some people say, "I must have one of those faces." What facial expressions indicate you are willing to listen? Have you ever been in line at the grocery store or sitting in the doctor's office when a complete stranger began talking to you and disclosed more than you expected for a first meeting? Does this happen to you regularly? If so, what sort of verbal and nonverbal messages might you be sending?

# Chapter 6
# Reflecting Skills I: Paraphrasing

**Chapter Summary**

While the invitational skills learned in the last chapters encourage the client to open up, reflecting skills communicate empathy, demonstrate understanding, and stimulate deeper exploration. The reflecting process involves repeating back to the client facts and feelings in a concise way. The best reflecting statements communicate both an accepting, nonjudgmental attitude and an accurate portrayal of the client's story.

All client messages include two parts, the factual content and the underlying feelings. Reflecting both facts and feelings allows the client to feel more completely understood. Helpers use <u>paraphrases</u> to summarize and reflect the content or facts in the client's story. Paraphrases are miniature versions of the story fed back by the helper to let the client know that essential information has been received. The greatest challenge in paraphrasing is in trying to reduce or distill the story into a few words.

**Glossary**

*Paraphrase*: A paraphrase is a distilled version of the content of the client's message. The content includes significant facts, thoughts, and intentions. Helpers use the skill of paraphrasing to allow clients to feel understood.

*Reflection of feeling*: A reflection of feeling (ROF) is a helping response that accurately identifies the clients' emotions based on their verbal or nonverbal messages.

**Video Exercises**
**Exercise 6A: Learning to Paraphrase**

Video segment titled *Paraphrasing* showed Samantha (the helper) demonstrating paraphrasing with Stacey (the client). Watch the whole segment first and then go back and look at specific parts as directed by the questions below. Here, and in later chapters, you are asked to identify skills by their names. Learning to identify helper responses will help you when you watch your own videos or go over your transcripts. It will also assist you in giving useful feedback to your fellow students since you will be using a common language. At other times, you will be asked to examine the client's response to the helper's intervention. Examining a client's reaction is one way to check the effectiveness of your statement. Did it achieve what you hoped? Did it confuse or silence the client?

1. Samantha used the skill of paraphrasing five times in this segment. See if you can identify the five paraphrases. Write them out in the space provided. Underneath each, indicate how the client reacted to the paraphrase. Did they tend to move the client along to the next part of the story?

Paraphrase 1:

_____

_____

Client reaction:

_____

Paraphrase 2:

_____

_____

Client reaction:

_____

Paraphrase 3:

_____

_____

Client reaction:

_____

Paraphrase 4:

_____

_____

Client reaction:

_____

Paraphrase 5:

_____

_____

Client reaction:

_____

2. Write down one door opener used by Samantha.

_____

_____

3. In this video, Samantha does not seem interested in Stacey's boyfriend. Why doesn't she ask about him? What effect do you think this might have had on the conversation?

_____

_____

_____

_____

4. After watching the video, try and write a one-sentence paraphrase, in your own words, that captures the major facts in Stacey's story.

_____

_____

**Exercise 6B: The Skill of Paraphrasing - Reflecting Content**

Listed are 5 client stories. Attempt to <u>paraphrase</u> the stories, reflecting the <u>content</u> of the information provided. Do not reflect feelings.

1. "Since my son came home after visiting with his father he has behaved very differently toward me. He has been having temper tantrums, refusing to do his chores and yesterday he cursed at me. I have tried time-outs but nothing seems to work with him."

Paraphrase:_____

_____

_____

2. "I was in the office as usual, doing my work, and I get this phone call from my boss. She asks me to come into her office then tells me she has to 'let me go'. I have always been a good worker, apart from that last review."

Paraphrase:_____

_____

_____

3. "My mother-in-law decided to buy the kids some computer games for Christmas— the violent ones. She knows how we feel about the children watching violent materials."

Paraphrase:_____

_____

_____

4. "I'm in trouble again with my teacher, Mrs. Henderson. She's always picking on me, even when I do nothing wrong. This time Alex poked me in the back with his ruler. Then she starts yelling at me. Like it was my fault or something."

Paraphrase:_____

_____

_____

5. "I had such big plans for my future. I'd been slowly putting money away in these great stocks. I planned to sell them this year, move to Colorado, and start a business selling my art. But now the market has crashed and I've lost everything. I have to give up all my plans."

Paraphrase:_____

_____

_____

## Exercise 6C: Making Your Paraphrases Nonjudgmental
The following client statements test your ability to be nonjudgmental - neither agreeing nor criticizing. Paraphrase the content of the following client statements without taking sides.

1. "I've just been released from the hospital, and my doctor says I have to come and see you. I think she wants me to leave my husband because of all these injuries and bruises. But it's really not his fault; it's me who sets him off. And besides it doesn't happen very often, only when he's had a few beers."

Paraphrase:_____

_____

_____

2. "I am so excited; I am getting married in 2 weeks. We met over the Internet and she just sounds great. Even though we've never met, I know she is the one for me. In fact we aren't going to meet before the wedding. Isn't it romantic?"

Paraphrase:_____

_____

_____

3. "I don't know whether to have this pregnancy aborted. The thing that worries me is that I've had 2 abortions in the past, and too many can affect your ability to have children in the future. I do want to have a family, just not right now. I have too much going on in my career."

Paraphrase:_____

_____

_____

Helpers often have difficulty not taking sides. Which of these situations would most challenge your ability to be nonjudgmental?

_____

_____

For what reasons? _____

_____

**Multiple Choice and Short Essay Questions**

1. Which of the following statements are paraphrases, reflecting content?
   a. You look a little uncomfortable.
   b. You feel lonely without them.
   c. I wonder what this experience was like for you.
   d. Your mother phones you twice a day.

2. Which statement is <u>most</u> accurate?
   a. It is important to side with the client when discussing a third party.
   b. It is important that reflections are nonjudgmental.
   c. Paraphrases should be 7 or 8 words at most
   d. A paraphrase is essentially a reflection of feeling

3. Which paraphrase is nonjudgmental?
   a. Your boss clearly has issues.
   b. Everyone has treated you very unfairly.
   c. In your opinion, Jack is not showing you enough affection.
   d. Jack is an unaffectionate person.

4. Briefly describe the four functions of reflecting skills in the helping relationship.

5. Identify two common problems associated with learning to paraphrase in the helping relationship. What techniques or strategies could you use to overcome these challenges?

**Journal**

Select one of the "starters" below to begin your journal for this chapter. Remember that starters are designed to warm you up to these issues. You may take them in whatever direction you like. You need not answer every question if they distract you from an important thought or stop the flow of ideas.

1.  Now that you have begun to practice some of the skills, how has this learning affected your feelings of confidence? Are you experiencing any of the anxiety or awkwardness that was predicted? If so, how are you coping with it? Do you have times when you feel comfortable with your work and other times when you lack confidence? What is different about these two times?

2.  Consider a time when someone listened to you in such a way that you felt heard and understood. How did this person communicate this understanding or empathy? What was the experience like for you? In what ways was the interaction helpful for you?

# Chapter 7
# Reflecting Skills II: Reflecting Feelings

## Chapter Summary
In contrast to paraphrasing, the skill of reflecting feelings focuses on the underlying or openly expressed emotions. Reflecting feelings is an important and challenging skill to master. In the beginning, students have difficulty with this skill because they wait too long to reflect, they use long and rambling reflections, and they tend to repeat the client's identical words, rather than rephrasing. Studying common reflecting errors can help students improve their reflections of feeling. Students should also review lists of emotional adjectives to improve their feeling vocabularies. With more precise words, helpers can communicate feelings more accurately. Written practice in identifying emotions in a client story is one of the most helpful beginning steps to reflecting feelings. In this guide, there are two video segments, *Reflecting Feelings I* and *Reflecting Feelings II*, demonstrating this skill. In addition there are several written exercises to help you begin to identify feelings and construct accurate reflecting responses.

## Glossary
*Reflection of feeling*: A reflection of feeling (ROF) is a helping response that accurately identifies the clients' emotions based on their verbal or nonverbal messages.

*Overshooting*: Overshooting is a common error of accuracy in reflecting feelings. It refers to a helper response that exaggerates the client's feeling beyond what the client is trying to communicate. For example, if a helper reflects anger when a client is only annoyed, the helper is overshooting.

*Undershooting*: Undershooting is also an error of accuracy in reflecting feelings. Undershooting is underestimating a client's emotion and reflecting a feeling that is too mild. For example, if a client is shocked and the helper says, "mildly surprised."

*Parroting*: Parroting is the error of reflecting feelings by repeating the client's exact words. A good reflecting response uses slightly different language.

## Written Exercises
## Exercise 7A: Recognizing Paraphrases and Reflections of Feeling
Classify the following statements as either a paraphrase (indicate "P") or a reflection of feeling (indicate "ROF"). Answers are given at the end of the chapter.

1. ___ You feel that your husband neglects you.

2. ___ You are wondering whether you are good enough.

3. ___ You looked sad when you mentioned your father.

4. ___ Your work sounds demanding.

5. ___ You sound positive and optimistic about this relationship.

6. ___ That must have been shocking for you.

7. ___ You feel he owes you a debt of gratitude.

8. ___ You miss them greatly.

9. ___ How disappointing.

10. ___ I imagine you were overjoyed.

**Exercise 7B: Learning to Identify Feelings: The First Step in Reflecting**

1. Listed below are the eight basic emotional states identified by your text. As you observe Margaret (the client) in the segment titled *Reflecting Feelings I*, which of these general emotional tones can you identify? Place a check next to the categories you hear. For each category that you checked, try to identify one <u>finer shade of feeling that Margaret could be experiencing.</u> For example, if anger is the category, a finer shade that the client might be feeling is resentment.

| Category | Observed? (Check) | Shade |
|---|---|---|
| a. Joy | ____ | _____ |
| b. Sadness | ____ | _____ |
| c. Anger | ____ | _____ |
| d. Guilt/Shame | ____ | _____ |
| e. Fear | ____ | _____ |
| f. Disgust | ____ | _____ |
| g. Surprise | ____ | _____ |
| h. Interest/Excitement | ____ | _____ |
| i. Weakness | ____ | _____ |
| j. Strength | ____ | _____ |
| k. General Distress | ____ | _____ |

2. Watch segment *Reflecting Feelings I* from 11:06-11:30. Stop immediately and write down the emotion that you think Margaret is feeling. Next, write a reflection of feeling (in your own words) based on the feeling you have identified.

_____

_____

_____

_____

3. Share your reflection of feeling with a fellow student. Write your reflection and your fellow student's reflection here. Compare your answers here and then discuss:

_____

_____

_____

_____

**Exercise 7C: Practice Identifying Feelings in Context**
1. In order to identify reflections of feeling, watch the entire video segment *Reflecting Feelings II* and write down each of the emotional states that Mark (the helper) identified in Lisa's (the client) story.

_____

_____

_____

_____

2. If you were Lisa, what additional feelings might you be experiencing?
This technique of imagining yourself as the client may help you identify the emotions that the client has not openly expressed but are hidden in the story.

_____

_____

_____

_____

3. At 15:16 Mark reflected the feeling of frustration and at 15:40, resentment. Since the client has not mentioned these feelings, review the tape and see if you can identify one or two nonverbal or verbal cues that led Mark to suspect these emotional states.

_____

_____

_____

_____

**Exercise 7D: Stretching Your Feeling Vocabulary**

For the following primary emotions list at least 5-7 alternative feeling words that describe this emotional state. Focus on a range of intensities, from mild to strong descriptions of these emotional experiences.

1. Anger: _____

_____

_____

_____

2. Sadness: _____

_____

_____

_____

3. Fear: _____

_____

_____

_____

4. Guilt/Shame: _____

_____

_____

_____

5. Joy: _____

_____

_____

_____

**Exercise 7E: Identifying Feelings in Client Statements**

Read the following client statements. Identify as many feelings as you can to reflect the client's emotions. Put yourself in the client's position and imagine the possible feelings he or she might be experiencing.

1. "I don't think I love my wife. She is a great mother and we get along well but there is no passion any more. And now I've met Susie and she is incredible, I can't get her out of my mind. I don't know what to do. I'm not the kind of man that does this. It's wrong but I can't help myself."

Feelings:_____

_____

_____

_____

2. "My parents disapprove of my boyfriend, they don't like his job, his appearance and also because he was married before. Now my mother tells me that they are going to cut me out of their will if I don't leave him."

Feelings:_____

_____

_____

_____

3. "I think my 14-year old son may be using drugs. He seems so different lately, kind of distant. His grades are terrible and he won't talk to me about it. The other day I went through his room, to look for any kind of evidence of drugs. I know I shouldn't have, but I really didn't have a choice. If he knew what I did he would be so mad."

Feelings:_____

_____

_____

_____

4. "I don't know what is wrong with me, ever since the boating accident. I can't seem to concentrate. I keep forgetting things, like appointments and where I've put things. Then I burst into tears yesterday for no reason. Sometimes I wonder if I'm going crazy!"

Feelings:_____

_____

_____

_____

5. "My girlfriend has a new job and wants me to cook dinner for her new boss and some work colleagues. I am so nervous. I know it won't be good enough and I'll let her down. I've always been shy and these people seem so important. I feel sick thinking about it."

Feelings:_____

_____

_____

_____

**Exercise 7F: More Practice in Identifying Specific Feelings**
Using the simple stem "You feel_____," create reflection of feeling statements that accurately mirror the client's feeling and the appropriate shade of intensity.

1. "I can't believe the way the company has treated me. Firing me after 25 years of service. It is outrageous."

    You feel_____ (specific emotion)

2. "My daughter seems so unhappy, she cries in her room for hours at a time. I just don't know how to help her, nothing I say makes any difference."

    You feel_____ (specific emotion)

3. "I can't believe that the university accepted my application to the graduate program. Not only that, they offered me a scholarship."

    You feel_____ (specific emotion)

4. "I trained so hard for the competition. I ran every day for a whole year. The week before I broke my leg and couldn't enter. "

    You feel_____ (specific emotion)

5. "The new man I've met is wonderful. I just know this relationship is going to better than any of the others."

    You feel_____ (specific emotion)

## Exercise 7G: Connecting Feelings and a Paraphrase

Using the stem "You feel_____ because _____," create statements that reflect feeling and the related reason, based on the content. Make your paraphrase brief. The word because must logically connect the feeling and the content. Number 1 is completed for you as an example

1. "My husband and I keep fighting. We argue over very minor things. I didn't really mind before, but I think its having a big impact on the kids."

   Reflection of feeling: <u>You feel worried because the disagreements seem to be unsettling for the kids.</u>

2. "I think my girlfriend likes someone else. Whenever I turn around, I see her talking to James. She seems to laugh a lot when I see them together."

   Reflection of feeling: _____

   _____

3. "I've always wanted to be an actor. But my mom and my teacher have told me it's a crazy idea and I need to get a proper job. Acting is all I want to do."

   Reflection of feeling: _____

   _____

4. "I told my best friend something that was top secret. I found out yesterday that she told my worst enemy in the whole school."

   Reflection of feeling: _____

   _____

5. "My sister's boyfriend is just terrible. He drinks too much and never works. I don't know, but I think he may be cheating on her."

   Reflection of feeling: _____

   _____

**Exercise 7H: Keeping the Focus on the Client while Reflecting Feelings**
In the following statements, the client focuses on someone else. Create reflection of feeling statements that reflect the client's emotions. Use the stem "You feel_____ because _____." Remember to neither judge nor take sides.

1. "My boyfriend has become more and more controlling. He criticizes me constantly, tells me who I can spend time with and the other day smashed my collection of ornaments because I came home late."

   Reflection of feeling: _____

   _____

   _____

2. "I can't stand my boss. She is condescending to me and has no managerial skills."

   Reflection of feeling: _____

   _____

   _____

3. "My mother treats me like a 4 year old child. Yesterday she phoned and reminded me to wear a warm coat in the cold weather. I am 27 years old."

   Reflection of feeling: _____

   _____

   _____

4. "This other girl in my class seems so lonely and unhappy. She has no friends and cries during the breaks between classes."

   Reflection of feeling: _____

   _____

   _____

5. "My boyfriend works all the time. He is never home. The few times he is home he falls asleep on the couch."

   Reflection of feeling: _____

   _____

   _____

**Self-Assessment**

Practice reflecting feelings with a fellow class member as the client. This practice can be as short as ten minutes. Following the practice session, ask your fellow student to fill out the following feedback directly into your workbook.

To the "Client":

Please respond as honestly as possible to the following statements, using the 5-point scale below:

| 1 | 2 | 3 | 4 | 5 |
|---|---|---|---|---|
| *Strongly Disagree* | *Disagree* | *Neutral* | *Agree* | *Strongly Agree* |

1. ___ The helper's nonverbals and opening skills seemed appropriate.

2. ___ The helper allowed me to talk too long before reflecting.

3. ___ The helper showed warmth.

4. ___ The helper's responses seemed concise.

5. ___ The helper seemed to understand the facts.

6. ___ The helper at times reflected using the original words I used (parroting).

7. ___ The helper identified one or two primary feelings accurately.

8. ___ The helper reflected a feeling of which I was unaware.

9. ___ Overall, the session helped me reflect a little more deeply about the situation.

Please identify one or two things the helper did well in the session

1._____

2._____

Please identify one or two things the helper can do to further improve his or her skills.

1._____

2._____

To the Helper:

Based on the feedback you received, identify one or two things you hope to work on in upcoming practice sessions.

1._____

2._____

**Multiple Choice and Short Essay Questions**

1. Which of the following statements is a paraphrase, reflecting content?
   a. You look a little uncomfortable.
   b. You feel lonely without them.
   c. I wonder what this experience was like for you.
   d. Your mother phones you twice a day.

2. Which of the following statements are reflections of feeling?
   a. You feel that he is no good for you.
   b. You are confused about which direction to take.
   c. Your wife neglects you.
   d. You feel you deserve better.

3. Which of the following statements is the <u>most</u> accurate?
   a. Parroting is recommended as it connects client and helper with common words.
   b. Reflecting feelings is relatively easy to learn.
   c. Reflecting feelings can deepen the helping relationship
   d. Reflect feelings in the form of questions is preferable, as it allows you to first check your perception with the client

4. Discuss the main differences between reflections of feeling and paraphrases. Give an example of each as if you were saying them to a client.

5. Identify and briefly describe 3 qualities of effective reflections of feeling.

**Journal**

Select one of the "starters" below to begin your journal for this chapter. Remember that starters are designed to warm you up to these issues. You may take them in whatever direction you like. You need not answer every question if they distract you from an important thought or stop the flow of ideas.

1. Think about the expression of emotion in your own family of origin. Do you think that some emotions were more allowable than others were? How do you think your own family or ethnic background might affect your willingness to listen to a client's feelings?

2. Think about the following negative emotions: sadness, anger, and fear. Do you think it is correct to call them "negative?" If a client expressed one of these feelings frequently and with great intensity, which ones would be the hardest for you to deal with? Why?

# Chapter 8
# Reflecting Meaning and Summarizing

**Chapter Summary**

The meaning of a client's story is its significance to them. The meaning of the story may include what it reflects about the client, their view of others, or view of the world. For example, being fired from a job can evoke strong feelings, but these feelings are different for each person based on his or her background. One person might believe that they are being treated unfairly and become angry, while another might blame himself or herself and feel ashamed.

Reflections of meaning are helper responses that go beyond the superficial and get at these implicit messages. Because clients are often unaware of the contribution of meaning to their reactions, the helper must use intuition to extract and show the client this hidden facet. When the helper reflects the facts, the feelings, and the meanings of a client's story, he or she feels that the helper has understood at a very deep level. In order to bring out meaning, helpers can use reflections of meaning or ask questions such as, "What do you value?" and "What about this bothers you so much?"

A second advanced reflecting skill is *summarizing.* Summaries pull together the content, feelings and meanings in a distilled form. Summaries are used at transitions in the helping session. At times they serve to focus the client on the major issues, identify themes, signal a change to a new topic, or serve to plan the next steps.

The Nonjudgmental Listening Cycle (NLC) is a way of explaining the sequence of skills that a helper normally employs as he or she explores a new topic with a client. The NLC roughly outlines the sequence from opening skills to reflecting skills to advanced reflecting skills, going deeper as the client discloses more (see chart in the Appendix). Understanding the NLC can help new learners decide which skills to use at various points in the initial stage of helping. By analyzing the NLC in transcripts or in classroom practice, a student can see the pattern of his or her responses and avoid the problem of overusing closed questions that keep the client focused on the more superficial aspects.

**Glossary**

*Worldview*: A term coined to refer to a person's view of self, others, and the world. These ideas come from culture, family, and ethnic background as well as the person's life experiences.

*Values*: These are assumptions about what is right and wrong. By understanding a client's values, we begin to grasp his or her internal struggles and moral dilemmas. Values are a person's basis for self-evaluation and the evaluation of others. A client's values tell us about what the client expects of himself or herself, how his or her ideals and aspirations are defined, and what is important to them.

*Reflecting Meaning*: Reflecting meaning is an advanced reflecting skill in which the helper feeds back to the client the underlying meanings based on the client's worldview and values.

*Summary*: A summary is a distilled version of facts, feelings, and meanings covering everything the client has said up to that point. Better summaries include all three domains.

*Focusing Summary*: The helper often uses this kind of summary in the beginning of a session to remind client and helper of previous sessions and goals. The focusing summary can also be used when it appears that the session has gotten off track.

*Signal Summary*: Helpers use signal summaries to send a message to the client that the story has been grasped. When clients receive a signal summary, they feel free to go on and explore other issues.

*Thematic Summary*: Sometimes the helper notices repeated experiences, feelings, and meanings in the client's story. A helper identifies a theme and feeds it back to the client.

*Planning Summary*: Helpers usually make planning summaries at the end of a session. This type of summary includes a capsule version of the story but also identifies agreed upon plans for future work.

*Nonjudgmental Listening Cycle*: The NLC is the author's way of mapping suggested helper responses in a typical suggestion, moving the client from factual issues to feelings and then to meanings. The NLC ends with a summary.

### Exercise 8A:  Reflecting Meaning

Reflecting meaning is a difficult skill. One way to improve your ability to identify meanings is to go back and watch other segments on the CD and see if you can sense the underlying significance of the client's story, their worldview, and their values.  Don't focus on the helper's statements because they are demonstrating other skills. Instead, listen carefully to the client. Sometimes clients give only small clues to the reason why the issue is so important. It is likely that you will identify some reasons that the helpers on the CD missed.

Remember that there are two ways to get at meaning: (a) Reflecting meaning by rephrasing the client's statement, indicating that you understand the values, worldview or hidden meanings in the client's words; and (b) asking a closed question of the client that elicits the client's values and meanings. In both of the video segments devoted to meaning, the helpers use both methods.

a.  The video segment titled *Reflecting Meaning I* shows a conversation between a helper, Mark, and a client, Santiago. Watch the entire segment and then respond to the following questions.

Mark uses a question early on to focus Santiago on the meanings. What is it?

_____

_____


Later, Mark reflects a value implied in Santiago's story. What is it?

_____

_____

_____

b. To get a sense of meaning, it is often useful to reflect feelings for some time before reflecting meaning. There is at least one significant feeling that the helper failed to identify. Of the following categories, which do you think Mark missed? Circle your first choice.

Sadness/ Depression          Anger                    Joy/Happiness

Fear/Anxiety                 Guilt/Shame              Interest/Excitement

Surprise                     Disgust

Suppose you had reflected this feeling. What meanings would it lead you to? In other words, knowing the client feels this way, what can you guess about why this is such a conflict?

_____

_____


c. The video segment titled *Reflecting Meaning II* shows Dayle, the helper, talking with Eve, the client. Before watching the entire segment, listen to Eve's first statement beginning at 24:20 and ending at 25:10. Try for a moment to put yourself in Eve's situation.

What feelings might you be experiencing?

_____

_____


Why might you be feeling this?

_____

_____

_____


Does the answer to the question above give you a possible clue to the meaning of this decision? Guess what might really be troubling her.

_____

_____

_____


Now listen to the remainder of the segment. Dayle asked a number of insightful questions that give Eve clues to the significance of this decision. List two questions that you think were especially useful in getting Eve to dig deeper

1._____

_____

2._____

_____

Later on, Eve mentions "baby showers." Could this be a clue to the meaning in the client's life? Write a question that you might ask to get at this.

_____

_____

## Exercise 8B: Identifying Components of a Summary

The video segment titled *Summarizing* shows Grant, a teacher, talking to his student Liza. Grant makes several paraphrases and a couple of longer summaries of what Liza said. In this exercise, rather than analyzing Grant's summary, try to construct a summary of your own by watching the entire segment and writing down the facts, feelings, and possible meanings and combining them in a more compact version.

Note the issues Liza is dealing with:

_____          _____

_____          _____

List all of the feelings that she has either expressed or implied:

_____          _____

_____          _____

_____          _____

_____          _____

In identifying possible meanings, consider why this time of life so upsetting to her and what she values. Write your response(s) below:

_____          _____

_____          _____

Briefly, Liza alluded to the fact that this is not a new experience for her. What recurring feelings or underlined emotional theme might this represent?

_____

_____

Write your summary exactly as you might say it to Liza:

_____

_____

_____

Now collapse your response even more. See if you can reduce it by half:

_____

_____

### Exercise 8C:  Components of a Summary

In this exercise, you will be looking at the summaries in the video segments, _Reflecting Meaning II_ and the _Nonjudgmental Listening Sequence_. You may want to watch these again to get a sense of the whole session.

In video segment _Reflecting II,_ Dayle summarized her session with Eve beginning at 31:27. Watch that summary and answer the following questions:

a.  Dayle's summary is brief. Does it capture the essence of the entire conversation? Are facts, feelings and meanings included?  If you do not think so, what would you add?

_____

_____

_____

b.  Of the summary types described in the book - focusing, thematic, signal and planning - how would you categorize Dayle's?

_____

In video segment, the _Nonjudgmental Listening Sequence_, Mark, the helper, talks with the Anna, the client, who has some concerns about her relationship. Mark's summary begins at 42:13. Respond to the following.

a.  Listen to Mark's summary and dissect it into the following pieces to see if it covers the main points of Anna's story:

What facts or content issues did Mark allude to? _____

_____

What feelings did Mark mention? _____

_____

What meanings did Mark include in the summary? _____

_____

Looking back over this list, write a summary in your own words including any key facts, emotions, or meanings that would enhance the summary.

_____

_____

_____

_____

_____

_____

**Exercise 8D:  Understanding the Nonjudgmental Listening Cycle (NLC)**
The Nonjudgmental Listening Cycle is a prototype or map of the helper's responses when exploring a new topic. Typically, the helper starts with opening skills such as minimal encouragers, door openers, open questions, and closed questions. As more of the story comes out, more paraphrases and reflections of feeling are used. Finally, the helper identifies and reflects meanings and eventually summarizes the topic before moving on.

Watch the segment *Nonjudgmental Listening Sequence,* and classify each helper response in one of the following categories: minimal encourager (ME), door opener (DO), open question (OQ), closed question (CQ), paraphrase, (P), reflection of feeling (ROF), reflection of meaning (ROM), and summary (SUM).

1. _____

2. _____

3. _____

4. _____

5. _____

6. _____

7. _____

8. _____

9. _____

10. _____

11. _____

12. _____

13. _____

14. _____

15. _____


Look over the response pattern above. Does the sequence above generally fit the NLC pattern going from opening skills to reflecting skills to advanced reflecting skills to summary?

_____


Why do you think this kind of progression is recommended?

_____

_____

_____


**Written Exercises**
**Exercise 8E: Practice in Reflecting Meaning**
For each of the three client statements below, write both a question that would evoke meaning and a reflection of meaning using the "You feel _____ (emotion) because _____ (meaning)." For example, "You feel guilty because you don't feel you put in as much effort as you could have." Share your answers with a fellow student. Modify your answers if your conversation suggests you should.

a. "Two years ago, I lost my best friend. It was the first time anyone close to me has died. He was visiting England on a semester abroad with the college when he walked out of a restaurant and collapsed on the street. They say he had a blood vessel burst in his brain that was probably weak from birth. They brought him back and had a funeral, but his parents live about five hundred miles away. They didn't invite any of his friends to the funeral. I went to see his grave, but it turned out to be a plaque in a mausoleum. It was as if he vanished. Hard to believe he really died. I often wonder if he knew how important he was to his friends."

Question:

_____

_____


Reflection of Meaning: _____

_____

_____

b. "On Friday, I told my parents I was going to a play at school, but a whole group of us went to Ron's party and it turned out his parents weren't home. There was a lot of drinking and people passed out. Actually, it was boring. So eventually a few of us left and started driving around. We were in Jennifer's car. So we stopped at a rest stop on the freeway and when I came out of the restroom, two of the guys had stolen about 20 of those orange cones and put them in the trunk and back seat. I had been drinking a little, too, but I was mad at them for getting me involved in that. When I woke up the next morning, I heard the cops picked up the guy who was driving after they dropped me off. They have to go to court and his parents are taking the car away."

Question:

_____

_____

Reflection of Meaning:

_____

_____

_____

c. "I went into Mrs. Redd's sixth grade classroom during recess and I accidentally tripped over the cord for the CD player. So Ronnie Combs told her I did it on purpose, and I got punished. When Mrs. Redd yelled at me I wasn't allowed to say anything. She's always been mad ever since my mom took me out of her class but it wasn't my fault. I wish I were in that class. Old people never listen."

Question:

_____

_____

Reflection of Meaning: _____

_____

_____

d. "I've been out of work for six weeks and every day I am trying hard to find a job. My girlfriend is supportive, but she must be thinking less of me. I know I do. We had a big fight when she tried to pay my car payment. It's hard for a man to accept that kind of help."

Question: 

_____

_____

Reflection of Meaning: _____

_____

_____


**Exercise 8F: Constructing a Nonjudgmental Listening Cycle**
After each client statement, there is space for you to write a specific response. Record your answer as if you were actually talking to the client. Your final response will be a summary. After you have completed the assignment, go back and look over your responses and indicate how they could be improved.

Jennifer, age 15, a high school sophomore, has problems with motivation. She is about to fail her social studies class, requiring her to attend summer school. Her main goal is to pass social studies, and you have agreed to help.

Identify an open question to start the interview: _____

_____

Jennifer: "That's all my Mom talks about. I am not studying as hard as she wants me too. But I can't sleep very well. So I sleep in class sometimes. It's really boring and I'm not going to need social studies, I am going to be a flight attendant. I can't wait until I get out of high school and can run my own life for a change."

Your paraphrase: _____

_____

_____

Jennifer: "It's like this all the time, people telling me what to do. I want to pass but I just can't sleep. Maybe if everybody would leave me alone. My friends are having trouble with Mr. Robinson, the social studies teacher. Everyone in the class is probably failing."

Your Reflection of Feeling: _____

_____

_____

Jennifer: "Yeah, that's how I feel. But why can't I be treated like an adult? At home, my Mom is always after me. She and my Dad are divorced. When I go to his house, he doesn't pressure me. He lets me do what I want. I would go and live with him but when I bring it up, he changes the subject. If they make me go to summer school, I will really be hard to live with. They have no idea."

Your Reflection of Meaning (use everything you've heard so far):_____

_____

_____

Jennifer: "The main thing is I have got to pass this class 'cause I can't handle the whole summer in school again. The summer is when you're supposed to go to the mall and the beach. If they make me go to summer school, I'll probably sleep in class."

Your Summary: _____

_____

_____

_____

_____

**Self-Assessment**

1. Looking over your CD and written practice, how well do you think you are able to identify and reflect meanings?

1    2    3    4    5    6    7    8    9    10

*No success*            *Occasionally I get it*        *Most of the time I hear the*
                                                          *deeper meanings*

2. Looking over your CD and written practice, how would your rate your summaries on the following three scales?

1    2    3    4    5    6    7    8    9    10

*Are too long and rambling*                  *Are concise capsules*

1    2    3    4    5    6    7    8    9    10

*Contain facts or feelings*                                    *Include meanings*

1        2        3        4        5        6        7        8        9        10

*Don't cover the whole story*                    *Summarize most of the key issues*

3. What do you need to work on? _____

_____

_____


**Multiple Choice and Short Essay Questions**

1.  It is important to reflect meaning because:
    a.  clients gain knowledge about themselves.
    b.  clients are able to set goals that are really important to them.
    c.  reflecting meaning helps a client feel understood at the deepest levels.
    d.  all of the above

2.  Meanings can be brought to a client's attention by:
    a.  reflecting
    b.  questioning
    c.  confronting
    d.  a and b

3.  Reflecting meaning is difficult because:
    a.  Helpers don't know how to reflect meaning or ask meaning-oriented questions.
    b.  Clients may not feel comfortable going so deep.
    c.  People take meanings for granted, assuming everyone sees the world as they do.
    d.  All of the above

4.  The text identified four different types of summaries. Identify these and explain when each should be used.

5. Construct a dialog between a helper and client in which the helper uses the Nonjudgmental Listening Cycle to explore a particular topic. Start with an open question; add door openers and minimal encouragers. Go on to paraphrase and later reflect feelings. The final responses should be reflections of meaning. Try and construct one that includes a reflection of meaning. Finish with a summary.

**Journal**

1. One of the ideas in this chapter is that a client's worldview, values, and experiences shape their construction of a problem. Think about a problem you are having right now. What values of yours influence the way you think and feel about the problem? Where did these values come from?

2. An often-used method for assessing client self-esteem is to ask him or her to identify some key strengths. Try this for yourself. See if you can list ten personal strengths and then react to these in writing. If you found this difficult, what cultural and familial values might be blocking you? How would you react to a client who could identify only one or two strengths?

3. Think about a strong personal value you hold and think about how you might react to a client who holds the opposite value. For example, let us say you value health and you encounter a client who smokes, drinks excessively, and takes other substantial health risks. In the value that you chose, under what circumstances would you confront the client or expose your own values? What ethical issues should concern you?

# Chapter 9
# Challenging Skills

**Chapter Summary**

This chapter looks at two important skills for providing the client with vital information. The first skill is feedback; presenting the client with your perceptions – what you see, feel, or suspect about him or her. Feedback should not be given on personality traits, rather, it is more effective to the degree that it is behavioral, specific, concrete, and nonjudgmental. Before giving feedback, ask the client's permission and be sure it is useful information and is presented in a way that the client can accept it. Don't forget that feedback about client strengths is also useful, as long as it does not fall into the category of praise (judgmental feedback).

Confrontation is one of the most powerful counseling techniques you will learn. It involves identifying discrepancies – things that do not fit together – in a client's story. Inconsistencies may include a smile that clashes with the sad story a client is telling or it may be between the client's career plans and his or her interests. The basic algorithm for the confrontational response is "On the one hand _____ and on the other, _____."

For example, "On the one hand you say you want to go see your mother, but every time in the last two months she has come to pick you up, you have other plans." A good confrontation is one that does not ignore the inconsistencies in a client's story and respectfully challenges the client to change.

Helpers should also observe the client's response to the challenge and determine if the client's attitude is (1) denial of a discrepancy; or (2) partial acceptance; or (3) complete acceptance. Based on the client's reaction, the helper can modify the confrontation so that it is becomes more palatable.

When a helper presents the client with a discrepancy, it may place some strain on the therapeutic relationship. Previously the client found the helper supportive and exploratory and now the helper is challenging the client's construction of the world. Confrontation if mishandled can send clients retreating to the safety of their defenses. Clients may even abandon the therapeutic process altogether. The helper must find a way to gently make clients aware of their inconsistencies without mortally wounding the therapeutic bond.

**Glossary**

*Feedback*: Providing another person with information about how you perceive him or her.

*Self-disclosure*: Revealing information about the self to others. Deeper self-disclosure is thought to lead to greater self-knowledge, self-acceptance, and deeper interpersonal relationships.

*Discrepancies*: Inconsistencies in thoughts, feelings, and behaviors in a client's story.

*Confrontation*: Presenting the discrepant elements of a client's story and asking the client to resolve the inconsistencies.

*Blind spot*: Things others know about us but we do not know about ourselves.

*Cognitive Dissonance*: Discomfort caused by possessing conflicting values, attitudes, and beliefs. We are motivated to reduce the dissonance by resolving or obliterating the differences.

*Helper Confrontation Scale*: A five-point scale that indicates how well the helper is able to deliver a challenging yet acceptable confrontation to a client.

*Client Acceptance Scale*: A three-point scale that reflects the client's acceptance of a confronting response.

### Video Exercises
There are two segments on the CD demonstrating confrontation. *Confrontation I* begins at 43:18 and *Confrontation II* begins at 48:00. These segments are longer because it takes some time before the helper can understand the conflict within the story before making an appropriate confrontation. Notice that the nonjudgmental listening cycle leads up to the confrontation.

### Exercise 9A: Analyzing Confrontations and Client Responses
The video segment entitled *Confrontation I* shows Mark (helper) and Nasundra (client) discussing her wedding plans. Watch this entire segment and answer the questions below.

At 46:13 Mark says, "I don't want to say this too strongly, but it sounds like you're more afraid of embarrassing your family than doing what you would like to do. . ." Watch this section and look at Nasundra's reaction to this confrontation. Make note here of any nonverbal communications that might signal the degree of her acceptance of Mark's confrontation.

_____

_____


Using the Client Acceptance Scale, how would you rate Nasundra's statement at 46:26 beginning with, "Um. Wow. . "

(1) Denial of Discrepancy   (2) Partial Acceptance   (3) Full Acceptance

What, in Nasundra's response, prompts you to make this assessment?

_____

_____

Using the Helper Confrontation Scale in the Self-Assessment Section later in this chapter, rate Mark's confrontation

1       2       3       4       5

Why did you give it this rating?

_____

_____

Twice Mark says, "I don't want to say this too strongly." What effect does this have on the confrontation?

_____

_____

Do you like this statement? Why or why not?

_____

_____

At 46:45 Mark uses the cliché, "You want your cake and eat it, too." Do you think this is too strong? How might you have responded instead?

_____

_____

What discrepancy is Mark trying to bring out at 46:45?

_____ vs. _____

What discrepancy is Mark trying to bring out at 47:16?

_____ vs._____.

**Exercise 9B More Work on Confrontation**
The video segment entitled, *Confrontation II* shows Dayle (helper) and Catherine (client) talking about Catherine's difficulty in completely stopping smoking. Watch the entire segment and then answer the questions below.

In the 95 seconds of the interview, Catherine talks about her dilemma (48:00 to 49:35). Based on this summary of the problem, what discrepancy (if any) do you see in her story?

_____

_____

At 49:37, Dayle identifies three discrepant elements in Catherine's story that form the basis of her conflict. How would you describe Catherine's reaction to Dayle's description? Does it push her to explore more deeply or does she become defensive?

_____

_____

70

At 52:10, Dayle says, "When you talk about that internal struggle, I notice you looked away. You looked a little sad." Is this a confrontation? If so, what are the discrepant elements? Is it merely feedback?

_____

_____

Write down all of Dayle's confrontations during this segment and rate each on the Helper Confrontation Scale (HCS) detailed in the Self-assessment section of this chapter.

Dayle's statement verbatim:                                      Your rating on the HCS

_____

_____

_____

_____

_____

_____

_____

_____

## Exercise 9C Giving Positive Feedback

It is easy to assume that people are aware of their strengths and we tend to focus on their foibles. More feedback is given to make people aware of weaknesses than their assets. Clients and even our own intimates need to know what is going right and what is working. Think about something that you like about a friend or colleague. Write down some positive feedback you might like to give.

_____

_____

Now, evaluate the feedback you gave according to the following criteria. Check those that apply.

1. Do not give people feedback on their personality traits.

2. Be specific, concrete, and nonjudgmental.

3. Ask permission before giving feedback.

4. Sometimes, feedback about touchy subjects is accepted more easily if it is offered tentatively. You do not have to dilute the feedback but rather, find an acceptable route to get the client to

think about what is being reported (This guideline may not be appropriate for this exercise, but it is useful to review it here).

5. Give only one or two pieces of feedback at a time.

6. Is this praise, a vague "pat on the head?"

What could you do to improve the kind of feedback you normally give?

_____

Give your friend or acquaintance the positive feedback using the guidelines and note his or her reaction here. How was it received?

_____

_____

What did you learn about how people receive feedback?

_____

_____

When giving negative feedback, to which of the guidelines above should you pay most attention?

_____

_____

**Exercise 9D Identifying Discrepancies**
This exercise gives you additional practice in "hearing" discrepancies in client problem situations. Write down the two warring sides. There may be more than one possible discrepancy. Record two, if you can.

1. "Robert is the most popular guy in the Junior class and he is in charge of the prom. Problem is that when we were freshmen, I beat him up after golf practice one day.  I can't even remember why. Proms are usually a complete waste of time because they have stupid music. But because of working for the alternative music magazine, I know a lot of people we could get to do the music for the prom. But I would have to go through him. So I am thinking of not going. That would be okay with me but my girlfriend is really excited about it."

_____ vs. _____

_____ vs. _____

2. "I just don't understand myself sometimes. I've had this boyfriend, Daniel for over a year. And it is fine, but sometimes when I am with him and my friends, I start flirting with other guys and I tell my girlfriends that Daniel and I are not that serious. I am not sure why I am this way, but when we are out together I don't want people to see us. When we are alone, we get along really well."

_____ vs. _____

_____ vs. _____

3. "The problem I have is that I have a big project to complete for my master's degree in Business Administration. But every time I sit down to work on it, I start surfing the Internet, playing some game on the computer. Once I get into it, I can spend several hours working on my thesis but half the time it is sheer torture just to sit there and go over that boring business stuff. Sometimes I wonder why I signed on to this thing. I do like business and am excited about the challenges ahead of me, but this project has nothing to do with my goals."

_____ vs. _____

_____ vs. _____

4. "My wife and I had always gotten along until I retired. Now, she treats me like I am just a problem getting in her way. She wants to go out, play cards and I am happy with the football games. I feel like I should have some fun. I don't see why you have to pay $2000 for a cruise to be happy. I remember when we used to be able to go for a walk or get ice cream and now she just looks at me and rolls her eyes. I never thought being retired would cause this kind of problem."

_____ vs. _____

_____ vs. _____

5. "Right now, I own my own dry cleaning business. I have 13 stores that pretty much run themselves. I go in for about 3 or 4 hours a day. The money has been unbelievable. I remember when I was in my 20s. All I wanted was to make money and to be a success, have people in the community think I was, you know, contributing. Now I am there and I am not sure it is enough. What happens when you achieve all of your goals? Where do you go? I feel I should be happy because there is nothing I am really lacking. Lately I have been drinking more than I should. Maybe I'm just bored."

_____ vs. _____

_____ vs. _____

**Exercise 9E Irrational Beliefs Exercise**

Not all discrepancies exist "inside the client's head." It is not only the client's thoughts and feelings that collide. Sometimes a discrepancy can exist between what is reasonable and what the client expects or wants. Many people find a conflict between what life really is and how they feel that it should be.

Albert Ellis identifies an irrational belief as a maladaptive way in which a person construes the world. It is a private conclusion that is irrational, and according to Ellis, "neurotic." One of the most common irrational beliefs is that "I must be loved and approved of by others almost all of the time." When stated this way, it sounds laughable; however, many of us subscribe to this idea to one degree or another. Ellis believes in confronting irrational expectations and adopting more reasonable ones. We can confront the irrational nature of a client's expectations by helping him or her to see how extreme they are. Read the client statements below. See if you can determine the inconsistency between the client's belief and a more reasonable expectation. One way of dealing with irrational ideas is to provide confrontation that exposes the client to their deeply held beliefs that conflict with reality.

1.  "I am a good student, with all A's this year. I also have a girlfriend and everything is going well in my life except for band. I am the worst trombone player in the band. The other people in there are band nerds so all they do is practice. I don't have time for that. I used to enjoy being in the band but it is hard when you are not one of the best."

    a.  Identify the client's belief:

    I must _____

    b.  Write down a more reasonable expectation.  I can reasonably expect:

    _____

    _____

    c.  Make a confrontation:  On the one hand you want _____ but on the

    other hand, it is more likely:  _____.

2.  "My problem is that I can't make a decision about whether to take this job or not. It is better pay than my present job. I have interviewed and even know two people who work there. But will it really pan out for me? I'd like the boss to tell me whether he thinks I can do the job to his satisfaction or not.  Also you hear about these telephone companies changing hands all the time. How do I know things will really stay the same?"

    a.  Identify the client's belief:

    I must _____

74

b. Write down a more reasonable expectation: I can reasonably expect:

_____

_____

c. Make a confrontation: On the one hand you want _____ but on the

other hand, it is more likely: _____.

3. "If it weren't for my family I could be happy. I can't even call over there without someone making me feel guilty. If I call my Dad, he says, 'Well, this is a special day.' -sarcastically. Then it ruins my whole day. And every year they go on a vacation to Myrtle Beach and I have to go along or everyone will be disappointed. And I don't like spending my whole time off at a place I've been before. I think they need therapy."

a. Identify the client's belief:

I must _____

b. Write down a more reasonable expectation: I can reasonably expect:

_____

_____

c. Make a confrontation: On the one hand you want _____ but on the

other hand, it is more likely: _____.

**Self-Assessment**
**Self-Assessment of Confrontation**
1. Go back and look at the exercises for this chapter. Indicate where you seem to be having the most difficulty. Circle Yes or No to the following questions.

I generally follow guidelines for giving good feedback.    Yes        No

Problems? _____

I can identify discrepancies in a client story.        Yes    No

Problems? _____

Sometimes I am judgmental when I point out discrepancies.   Yes   No

Problems? _____
I can point out discrepancies in a way that is acceptable to the client.   Yes   No

Problems? _____

2.  The Helper Confrontation Scale
Take a look at the Helper Confrontation Scale below. Based on your practice with fellow students, indicate the highest level you think have reached.

_____

Give an example of a confrontation that you have made either in practice or in the written exercises that you think would indicate a level 5 confrontation.

_____
_____
_____
_____

## Helper Confrontation Scale (HCS)

At level 1.0, the helper overlooks or accepts discrepancies, inconsistencies, or dysfunctional expressions of the client, or uses a harsh, abrasive or "put down" confrontation style.

At level 2.0, the helper does not focus on discrepancies but responds with silence or reflects without noting the inconsistency. This category also includes poorly timed confrontations.  For example, a strong confrontation that is delivered in the first few interchanges between helper and client, before a therapeutic relationship is established.

At level 3.0, the helper focuses attention on a discrepancy by questioning, or by pointing out the inconsistency. At level 3.0, the timing is appropriate and the confrontation is not abusive. For example the helper points out, that the client's verbal and nonverbal messages do not match.

Level 4.0 involves a direct confrontation by the helper.  It includes a challenge to the client to modify the behavior or to resolve the inconsistency, while at the same time protecting the client's self-esteem. To guard the client's self-esteem, the helper uses a nonjudgmental tone and a tentative approach.

Finally, level 5.0 includes all of the positive characteristics of the lower levels but is conveyed by the helper in a caring and helpful way along with enthusiasm for the client's growth.

**Multiple Choice and Short Essay Questions**

1. Receiving feedback is an important tool for personal growth because:
   a. it increases self-disclosure
   b. it increases what others know about us
   c. it decreases our blind spots
   d. all of the above

2. Good feedback involves all of the following except:
   a. It is specific.
   b. It is delivered more as a hint than a direct statement.
   c. A checking question is used to see if the person understands.
   d. On touchy subjects, it is delivered tentatively.

3. Cognitive dissonance is:
   a. The tendency not to bring up problems to others.
   b. A state of internal conflict caused by inconsistent thoughts.
   c. Lack of motivation when confused about what to do.
   d. When the client realizes there is a discrepancy and admits it.

4. The Helper Confrontation Scale evaluates a helper's ability to confront while the Client Acceptance Scale tests a client's willingness to accept a confrontation. What helper behaviors are most likely to lead to acceptance of a confrontation? How do we know when a client has really heard and accepted a confrontation?

5. List and describe each of the four steps in delivering an effective confrontation.

**Journal**

Read each journal item and then reflect in writing. You need not respond to every question in the journal starters below, instead, use them as stimuli to think about the issue.

1. Identify three or four major crises you have had in your life. What conflicts were you experiencing internally? See if you can see any patterns or themes to these conflicts. For example, do your conflicts seem to revolve around doing what you want to do versus doing what others want?

2. How comfortable are you with bringing up difficult issues with friends and family? Do you tend to be more tactful or more confrontational? When you go overboard, which end of the continuum do you approach? Are you too strong or too polite? Where might this tendency have originated?

3. Carl Rogers said that the greatest harm one can do to the self is to deny one's own thoughts, feelings and perceptions in order to gain the love of another. Reflect on Rogers' idea. Can you think of an example of when you were not true to yourself in order to stay in the good graces of others? How do you think you might have responded to a confrontation that highlighted the discrepancy between your actions and what you truly believed? How important do you think it is for a helper to confront clients when they are not being true to themselves?

# Chapter 10
# Assessment Skills

## Chapter Summary

The assessment stage of the helping process is the next step after the groundwork for a therapeutic relationship has been laid. Following assessment, helpers learn to develop treatment plans as clients set goals (step three). In the fourth step, helpers implement techniques and treatment plans and clients act to change their situations. In step five, client and helper evaluate the effectiveness of the helping process and plan for further changes or termination. Although entire courses are offered on the topic of assessment, the topic is introduced here so that students can understand how assessment fits into the selection of basic skills. Assessment is an important part of helping because it:

- Gives Crucial Information to Plan Useful and Realistic Goals
- Helps Clients Discover Events Related to the Problem
- Helps Us Recognize the Uniqueness of Individuals
- Uncovers the Potential for Violence Towards Self or Others
- Reveals Critical Historical Data
- Can Highlight Strengths, Not Just Weaknesses and Pathology
- Helps Clients Become Aware of Important Problems They Have Disregarded
- Keeps The Helper Focused on the Most Important Areas

In this chapter, four basic assessment methods are described: observation, questioning, the use of the genogram, and completing an intake form. In addition, the mental status examination is described briefly for two reasons. First, it is still widely used for gaining a general feel for the client, and second, the language of this examination is important to acquire so that one may communicate with a variety of other clinicians.

Observation involves noticing and recording helper impressions of the client. The genogram, questioning, and the intake form, on the other hand, involve give-and-take between helper and client. Observation is the art of paying attention to the client's speech, clothing, grooming, posture, build, gait, facial expressions, and general appearance. In addition, the helper needs to attend to his or her own feelings to see what the client evokes in him or her. The helper uses observation to make inferences about the client that might help in devising an appropriate treatment plan or open up areas of inquiry that the client is unwilling or unable to share. The helper should try to avoid cultural encapsulation that tends to mistakenly categorize clients based on stereotypes.

Questioning is an important skill for gaining information about client problems. It is appropriately used in the assessment phase when key background data is needed. The genogram is a graphic method for uncovering important family information including medical issues, substance abuse patterns, violence in the family, career expectations, family rules, roles, and rituals. Finally, completing an intake form is a standard assessment tool used by most helpers. It is a useful tool to make sure you are not missing something of vital importance. The ABC 1234 intake method is described in this chapter. This method makes sure you get crucial information about the client's affective, behavioral and cognitive functioning while gathering data concerning: (1) the client's developmental level, (2) the family history, (3) multicultural background, and (4) physical challenges and strengths. In our version of the intake form, we have included "Trigger Questions" as a training device. If the answer to any of these crucial questions is **"Yes",** you are encouraged to contact a supervisor for consultation.

**Glossary**

*Assessment*: Assessment is the general name for the interaction between client and helper wherein the helper is eliciting and recording data and the client is providing it. This can be achieved through conversation, observation, the use of assessment instruments and formal testing.

*Testing*: The formal process of testing involves assessment using standardized instruments such as an intelligence test.

*Diagnosis*: Diagnosis is the placing of a client's personality, symptoms, or problems into a category so that appropriate treatment can be applied. Normally, the term refers to a category in the DSM-IV list of mental disorders.

*Treatment Planning List*: This is a simple list of the client's problems in priority order.

*Observation*: Observation involves noticing and recording a client's verbal and nonverbal behaviors as these provide information that might be useful in helping the client.

*Cultural Encapsulation*: Cultural encapsulation is the tendency to view the client and the client's problems exclusively through one's own cultural lens without taking into account the client's background.

*Affect*: Affect is the outward manifestation of a client's emotions. Affective is used in this book to denote those emotional excesses and deficits that should be noted during the assessment process.

*Cognitive*: Cognitive refers to thinking. When assessing cognition, one must record the content of the client's thoughts. For example, is the client thinking negatively? Or is the client delusional? The helper must also consider if there is any biological disruption of thought processes due to illness or injury.

*Developmental*: Developmental issues are those that are common to a particular period of life. By assessing the client's stage of life, one can identify expected obstacles and resources for helping a client.

*Intake Form*: An intake form is the paper work a helper completes after seeing the client for the first time. Intakes normally record contact and demographic information, a brief notation about the client's problems, historical data, and a preliminary diagnosis.

*Genogram*: The genogram is a pictorial family tree that can elicit useful information about the client's family and cultural background.

**Video Exercises**
**Exercise 10A: Using Questions for Assessment**
Questions are an important method for gaining information about insight into the extent of a client's problems. Watch the segment entitled *Confrontation II* again and answer the questions that follow. *Confrontation II* begins at 48:00 showing Catherine (a client) and Dayle (the helper). In this segment Catherine talks about her problems with smoking. It would appear that an assessment of Catherine's current smoking behavior and her desired goals would be appropriate. Write three questions you would like to ask Catherine. Make sure your questions shed some light on the problem itself rather than merely satisfying your curiosity.

a. _____

b. _____

c. ._____

Of all the questions you have considered, which one is most likely to reveal crucial information?

_____

_____

How important is it to gain specific data about a client's troublesome behaviors? For example, would you have asked Catherine to record the number of cigarettes she smokes? Why or why not?

_____

_____

Catherine mentions something about her father. What relevance does this have to her problem? Is it worth exploring? If so, how might you do so?

_____

_____

_____

_____

**Written Exercises**
**Exercise 10B: Constructing a Genogram**:
Draw a genogram for a client named Bren using the instructions in Chapter 10 of your text. Bren is the second of three children. His parents, Tina and David, are both still living. He has always had a difficult relationship with his father whom he feels he can not please. His mother, Tina, is supportive and has a better relationship with Bren than she has with her husband. Bren has a strained relationship with his older sister, Heather, (age 32) and a closer relationship with his younger sister, Laura, age 28. Bren is 31 and has come to individual counseling because he is about to lose his job as a salesman. Bren says he does not like being a salesman but has never considered another line of work. He is avoiding his boss as much as possible because he is afraid the boss will want some concrete plans for improvement. He is having trouble with his wife who feels he is unmotivated. She wants to quit work to stay with their 2-year-old daughter, Muthoni. They have been married for 3 years. Bren does not tell his wife much about how he feels or thinks. They seldom fight and when they do, Bren just leaves the house and goes to see his parents for a few hours. Bren is unhappy, but he is most upset about the pressure from his boss and wife and is not sure how to handle either relationship. Draw Bren's genogram. For simplicity, we will omit Bren's grandparents from consideration.

Suppose Bren had been transferred to you from another helper. What issues do you think would be most important for you to explore? List three issues below and indicate why you would take time to further assess these areas.

1.  A question I might ask:

_____

_____

Why?

_____

_____

2.  A question I might ask:

_____

_____

Why?

_____

_____

3.  A question I might ask:

_____

_____

Why?

_____

_____

As you look at the questions you have elected to ask, evaluate each of them below. Indicate on a ten-point scale how important the question is. A "10" would represent a crucial question which unasked might lead to improper or inadequate treatment. A "1" on the scale indicates that you have asked the question more out of curiosity than out of necessity or relevance to the client's goals.

Question 1:          1     2     3     4     5     6     7     8     9     10

Question 2:            1      2      3      4      5      6      7      8      9      10

Question 3:            1      2      3      4      5      6      7      8      9      10

**Exercise 10C: "In Basket" - "Out Basket" Exercise**
It is important to distill assessment data into a set of major issues which can be placed on a problem list or "In Basket."  When a list has been compiled, the helper arranges the issues in order of importance and places the list in an "Out Basket."  Items arranged in the "Out Basket" list represent a treatment plan or goals placed in priority order. Consider the following issues in a client's "In Basket." Arrange them in the order that you would address them in an "Out Basket" list.

- The client wishes to develop a better relationship with his two children who live with his ex-wife.
- The client is a recovering alcoholic but has not been attending support group meetings.
- The client has been experiencing mild depression.
- The client has difficulty with his supervisor and is considering changing jobs.
- The client has an interest in drawing and painting and would like spend more time on artistic endeavors.
- The client indicates he feels lonely and isolated since his divorce one year ago.

In the spaces below, first list all of the client's issues that you might want to work on.  Next place them in the order you would address them. One guide for treatment planning is to think about Maslow's hierarchy of needs. Maslow suggested that basic physiological issues such as food, clothing, and shelter must be dealt with before higher needs such as belongingness, love, and self-actualization.

| In Basket | Out Basket (ordered by importance) |
|-----------|-----------------------------------|
| 1._____ | 1._____ |
| 2._____ | 2._____ |
| 3._____ | 3._____ |
| 4._____ | 4._____ |
| 5._____ | 5._____ |
| 6._____ | 6._____ |

Indicate why you gave Out Basket item #1 the highest priority.

_____

_____

Which issues, if improved, might have a generalized positive effect on the other areas of life? Should these be elevated on the list?

_____

_____

**Self Assessment**
In reviewing my assessment skills, I feel I need more work on (check all that apply):

1. Using questions
2. Observation
3. Working with a genogram
4. Interviewing and recording information
5. Using Tests

For those items that you checked, indicate how you might gain additional experience or training:

Observation

_____

_____

Working With A Genogram

_____

_____

Using Questions

_____

_____

Using Tests

_____

_____

**Cultural Encapsulation:**
Think for a moment about the population that you hope to work with in the future. Define the population either by ethnicity or culture, problem area (such as couples problems), or developmental level (such as children). Answer the following questions:

**How certain are you that you would enjoy working with this group of people?**

1    2    3    4    5    6    7    8    9    10

Uncertain                                                    Very certain


**How familiar are you with this population?**

1    2    3    4    5    6    7    8    9    10
Just beginning to know this population     Several years of experience

Think for a few minutes about how this group might vary. For example, if you chose children, could you also have children with a wide variety of ethnic backgrounds, learning disabilities, or physical handicaps?  What preparation should <u>you</u> make in your training to become more aware of assessment issues with this population?

_____

_____

_____

_____

_____

_____

**nal**

Think back on assessment experiences in your own life. These may range from encounters with a high school guidance counselor, to an intake interview at the college counseling center, or a College Board examination. What important decisions have you made based on testing or assessment results? What decisions have others made about you based on testing? Discuss any negative or positive experiences. How do these affect your views and feelings about testing clients?

This chapter suggests asking clients about religious and spiritual beliefs. How important are these issues to you? How often have you been able to discuss this part of your life with others? If you tend to hide this part of yourself, how do you think this affects others? How do you think others might react if they knew your religious or spiritual beliefs? If you were a client, how important would it be to discuss spirituality? If your spiritual or religious beliefs are not very well developed, how would you want a helper to approach this area?

Before you read the second paragraph of this journal starter, write a few sentences in reaction to the following statement: "Who am I?" Start by writing:

am_____. Try to record at least ten answers to this question.

This activity, "Who am I," is a standard journal activity often suggested by those who use journals for personal growth and self-awareness. As you read over this list of self-descriptors what are you aware of? Did you mention gender, occupation, or role (father, mother, sister, uncle)? Did you describe yourself as American or coming from some cultural or minority background? Are the things you mentioned first the most important? What does your list say about the way you view yourself? Could a self-assessment technique like this be of any use to a client or for a helper to understand more about a client?

**Multiple Choice and Short Essay Questions**

1. Cultural encapsulation refers to
   a. a summary of the client's ethnic heritage
   b. a client's ability to fit within mainstream culture
   c. a helper's tendency to see things through his or her own cultural len
   d. provincial attitudes of clients that keep them from changing

2. Testing can be a useful assessment tool. Which of these is a drawback?
   a. Formal testing **is** time-consuming and may not reveal more than the
   b. Few tests exist that measure family relationships
   c. They may be culturally biased
   d. All of the above

3. Diagnosis is a(n):
   a. highly accurate method for categorizing client problems
   b. way of simplifying all of the incoming information about the client
   c. activity that includes both client and helper
   d. technique only used by medical personnel

4. Identify five reasons for spending time in the assessment phase of helpi
   goals with a client.

5. Asking too many questions can be an error. When are questions helpful
   hinder?

6. List and describe five areas of a client's life you might assess using a ge

# Chapter 11
# Goal Setting Skills

## Chapter Summary

Goal setting is the third step in the stage of the helping process. The relationship-building and assessment phases precede it. The goal-setting process involves narrowing the focus of the helping dialogue to a smaller range of manageable units. Two useful skills for this "narrowing" process are <u>focusing on the client</u> and <u>boiling down the problem</u>.

Many clients complain of others as the problem in their lives. At the heart of their stories is the expectation and the hope that other people should change. Respectfully bringing the client back to his or her own experiences helps the client take responsibility and ownership for change. This is the technique of focusing on the client.

The process of boiling down the problem involves summarizing the overall session using reflecting skills, asking closed questions to prioritize concerns, selecting a smaller portion of the problem to work on, changing the problem to a goal, and defining the final goal statement. By boiling down the problem, helper and client transform an amorphous problem into manageable pieces. The process of developing realistic goals activates the expectation that the client's problems are solvable.

The purpose of the focusing on the client and boiling down the problem is to develop constructive goals in concert with the client. Constructive therapeutic goals are, mutually agreed upon by client and helper; specific, clear and easily restated; realistic; conducive to general improvement in the clients life; and address crises first. An important question to ask in the development of goals is "How will we know when we are finished?" Helping clients envision their ideals promotes goal-attainment and nourishes hope.

## Glossary

*Boiling Down the Problem*: This skill involves reducing the problem into several sub-problems and then further distilling it into a simple clear goal statement.

*Focusing on the Client*: Focusing on the client is the skill of responding to the client by emphasizing the parts of the story that relate to the client's experience rather the actions of other people or the environment.

*Treatment Planning*: Treatment planning is the helper-guided activity of selecting effective treatments for agreed-upon goals.

*Baseline*: Baseline refers to the numbers of a behavior that a client wants to increase or decrease. This is the number at the beginning of treatment against which change can be measured.

*Problem Ownership*: Problem ownership refers to the degree to which a person feels responsible for change. If a client "owns" a problem, he or she is disturbed by the situation and wants to make changes.

*Frequency*: One way of determining a change in behavior is to note the number of times it occurs. When we have identified the frequency, we can set a goal to increase or decrease the frequency of the behavior.

*Duration*: The amount of time a behavior is performed. Some client goals involve increasing the duration of a new behavior or decreasing the duration of a negative behavior. For example, a shy 15-year-old boy may set a goal of talking to a classmate for two minutes.

*Intensity*: Intensity is normally a subjective measure of discomfort measured in units of 1-10 or 1-100. A client might set a goal of being able to reduce anxiety from 80 to 60 using relaxation techniques.

**Video Exercises**
**Exercise 11A: Keeping the Focus on the Client**
Review the video segment entitled, *Nonjudgmental Listening Sequence*. The client and helper begin their discussion at 37:52 and end at 43:06, according to the counter on the screen. Mark (the helper) attempts to focus on the client, Anna, rather than her boyfriend.

a. List one helper statement that keeps the client focused on herself when the conversation could easily have moved to a discussion of her boyfriend's insensitivity.

_____

_____

_____

_____

b. Do you think that it would have been productive to say, "It sounds like your boyfriend doesn't try to make you feel comfortable at these parties"? Why or why not?

_____

_____

_____

_____

**Exercise 11B: Making the Transition to Goal Setting and Treatment Planning**
It is often difficult to know how to make the transition from the nonjudgmental listening sequence to goal setting and treatment planning. Review the video segment called, *Reflecting Meaning II*. (24:15-31:55). How does Dayle (the helper) help Eve (the client) begin focusing on goals? Identify two helper statements that nudge the client in this direction.

_____

_____

_____

_____

_____

**Exercise 11C: Boiling down the Problem.**

In the CD, few of the segments are long enough to show the entire process of boiling down the problem. Some time is required before the helper knows enough about client concerns to begin "narrowing." Review the video segment called, *Summarizing* (32:22-36:52). Identify three responses that Grant (the helper) could have made which might have moved Liza (the client) toward establishing a goal.

_____

_____

_____

_____

_____

_____

_____

_____

**Exercise 11D: Changing Problems to Goals**

One aspect of goal setting is changing problems to goals. A goal is not what one is lacking but something positive – how one wants things to be. Review the video segment, on *Nonverbal Skills* (00:47-03:10). Identify one goal, stated in the positive (not the absence of something), that might be appropriate for Kevin, the client.

_____

_____

_____

_____

_____

**Written Exercises**
**Exercise 11E: Focusing on the Client**

Create helper responses to the following client statements that focus on the <u>client</u>, not on another person or the environment. The responses may be reflections, open questions, or closed questions that shift attention back to the client's experience and perceptions.

1. Client: "My brother is an alcoholic who neglects his children. Those kids need a more loving father."

   Helper (client-focused) response:

   _____

   _____

   _____

   _____

2. Client: "If it weren't for my family, life would be perfect."

   Helper (client-focused) response:

   _____

   _____

   _____

   _____

3. Client: "My husband is the one who needs to be here. He destroyed our marriage and left me with nothing."

   Helper (client-focused) response:

   _____

   _____

   _____

   _____

4. Client: "I can't stand my co-workers. They are rude and inconsiderate. They never invite me to lunch with them."

   Helper (client-focused) response:

   _____

   _____

   _____

   _____

5. Client: "I deserve a pay raise. My company is so tight-fisted with money, they don't appreciate my talents."

   Helper (client-focused) response:

   _____

   _____

   _____

   _____

6. Client: "My mother is so domineering, she controls my life. She needs to back off!"

   Helper (client-focused) response:

   _____

   _____

   _____

   _____

7. Client: "This country's economy is to blame for my problems. It won't let anyone get ahead in life."

   Helper (client-focused) response:

   _____

   _____

   _____

   _____

8. Client: "My teacher hates me. She is the reason I got thrown out of school."

   Helper (client-focused) response:

   _____

   _____

   _____

   _____

9. Client: "I was abused as a child, not physically, but verbally. My parents were never there for me."

    Helper (client-focused) response:

    _____

    _____

    _____

    _____

10. Client: "My child is out of control. He is having temper tantrums ever since his father left."

    Helper (client-focused) response:

    _____

    _____

    _____

    _____

## Exercise 11F: Identifying Constructive Goals

Constructive goals are: mutually agreed upon by client and helper; specific, clear and easily restated; realistic, conducive to general improvement in the client's life, and address crises first. Assuming that the helper is in agreement, which of the following statements reflect the characteristics of constructive goals? Indicate the goals that you consider are constructive with a "C".

1. ____ I want to feel better about myself, you know, not really listening to other people at all.

2. ____ I want to develop two new friendships.

3. ____ I will take better care of my body by exercising three times per week and eating nutritional foods.

4. ____ My husband will speak to me nicely.

5. ____ I want more self-esteem.

6. ____ I want to set limits and consequences with my children at least 80% of the time they misbehave.

7. ____ I want to be happier.

8. ___ I want to attend counseling for three sessions to get my probation officer off my back.

9. ___ I want to ask a woman out on a date.

10. ___My family criticizes me and I want them to stop.

11. ___I want to stop my brother from using drugs.

12. ___I want to resolve conflict with my spouse in a new way, without name-calling.

13. ___I will to learn relaxation strategies so I can speak in public without shaking.

14. ___I want to persuade my ex-girlfriend to come back to me.

15. ___I know I have a drug problem, but I want to get myself squared away financially first.

## Exercise 11G: Developing Constructive Goals

In this exercise, you will attempt to write constructive goal statements for each of the client situations described below. The information provided is limited, so use your imagination to fill in the gaps. After each goal is a list of the criteria for a constructive goal. Check to see how well your goal matches these criteria.

1. Situation: The client, Sue, has been depressed for over a year since her divorce. She has limited social interaction with family and friends, and has stopped playing tennis, which she used to enjoy. Sue came for help to alleviate her depression and to regain her enthusiasm for these activities again.

   Goal:

   _____

   _____

   _____

   _____

   Circle those that apply:

   specific, clear, easily restated                    realistic
   conducive to general improvement in the clients life      address crises first

2. Situation: Mike came to see his helper due to problems managing his anger. He loses his temper with his wife, often yelling at her during disagreements over minor issues. His wife is considering separation. Mike wants to learn anger management and conflict resolution skills.

Goal:

_____

_____

_____

_____

Circle those that apply:

specific, clear, easily restated                                     realistic
conducive to general improvement in the clients life        address crises first

3. Situation: Jack is doing poorly in school, and his grades have dropped to "D's." He has difficulty paying attention for long periods and often gets out of his chair at inappropriate times. Jack and his parents want him to behave appropriately in class and get at least "B" grades at school.

Goal:

_____

_____

_____

_____

Circle those that apply:

specific, clear, easily restated                                     realistic
conducive to general improvement in the clients life        address crises first

4. Situation: Lucy is very shy and has difficulty making friends. Since moving to a new town 6 months ago she has developed no friendships and is feeling lonely. She would like to increase her confidence so she is able to initiate and maintain some friendships.

Goal:

_____

_____

_____

_____

Circle those that apply:

specific, clear, easily restated                                    realistic
conducive to general improvement in the clients life         address crises first

5.  Situation: Mary hates her job and in considering returning to school to change her career. Mary is confused about which direction of study to follow as her work experience and knowledge of careers is limited. She wants to pursue a career path that is personally fulfilling.

Goal:

_____

_____

_____

_____

Circle those that apply:

specific, clear, easily restated                                    realistic
conducive to general improvement in the clients life         address crises first

**Self-Assessment**
On a scale from 1-10 (1 = just beginning and 10 = mastery) indicate how well you think you have developed the skill of keeping the focus on the client. When answering, think about your practice sessions as well as your answers to the exercises in this chapter.

1       2       3       4       5       6       7       8       9       10

Indicate how well you think you are able to narrow the client's story to simpler goals or "boil down" the problem.

1       2       3       4       5       6       7       8       9       10

Now rate yourself on your ability to write constructive goals:

1       2       3       4       5       6       7       8       9       10

State two things you feel that you were able to improve upon this week. Recall feedback from fellow students or instructors. Include all feedback even if it does not relate to the skills of this chapter.

1.


2.


Which skills are you finding to be the most difficult to understand and practice?

_____

_____

_____

_____


Identify 2 steps you can take to help you improve your skills further. Identify concrete actions you are willing and able to take.

1._____

_____

_____

_____


2._____

_____

_____

_____

**Multiple Choice and Short Essay Questions**

1.  Which of the following statements is most accurate?
    a.  Goals should be broad and wide-ranging so as not to restrict the client.
    b.  It is primarily the helper's job to decide on the therapeutic goals.
    c.  A complex problem requires complex goals.
    d.  Constructive goals focus on the client rather than others.

2.  Which of the following statements meets the most criteria for a constructive goal?
    a.  My husband will attend Alcoholics Anonymous meetings regularly.
    b.  I will engage in social activities with friends at least twice a week.
    c.  I want to be less depressed.
    d.  People will like me.

3.  Which of the following helper responses is focused appropriately on the client?
    a.  Your son is very critical of you.
    b.  You feel threatened by your boss.
    c.  It sounds like he doesn't care about you.
    d.  Why does she behave that way?

4.  Outline three reasons why goal setting is an important aspect of the helping relationship.

5.  Briefly describe the characteristics of constructive goals.

**Journal**

1. Make a list of goals you would like to achieve in the next five years. Now, look at your goals and indicate what you think might keep you from accomplishing each one. Do you notice any personal unwillingness to think about this issue? Does it raise any anxiety? Discuss your reaction.

2. Imagine that you are a very old person talking to your relatives about your life. What were the major things you enjoyed in your life? Don't just recount your accomplishments but focus instead on those times when you were the happiest. It has been suggested that successful people are those who "follow their bliss." What things have you discovered that you really like to do? How can you incorporate them more into your present life? How can you use them to motivate yourself? What use can you make of this when you are trying to help another person?

3. Consider a personal problem that is currently troubling you. Respond to the following question "How will I know when the problem is gone?" Reflect on what will you be doing differently and what others will notice different about you. How will you feel when the problem is gone? Comment on this exercise. How might this process be helpful in goal setting?

# Chapter 12
# Solution Skills

**Chapter Summary**

Solution skills challenge the client to find answers to their problems. Some basic solution skills include giving advice, giving information, brainstorming, and alternate interpretation. These basic solution skills are the final building blocks you will learn. Later chapters focus on more advanced skills associated with the therapeutic factors, such as enhancing efficacy and self esteem, practicing new behaviors, lowering/raising emotional arousal, activating client expectations, hope and motivation, and providing new learning experiences.

Advice giving is a skill to be used sparingly if at all. There are special dangers for new helpers who tend to rely on this rather than helping clients explore their own solutions. Experienced helpers are reluctant to give advice because it undermines the client's self-confidence, it is rarely heeded, and it can conflict with the client's background and the cultural context of the problem.

Brainstorming is a group technique to stimulate creative thinking. It can be used as a method to generate new ideas when client and helper are engaged in problem solving. Alternative interpretation, on the other hand, is a method whereby the client is asked to question his or her assumptions about the problem. He or she is then asked to consider whether there are other possible ways of looking at the situation besides his or her first impression. Both methods are designed to broaden the client's perceptions about problem situations and stimulate creative responses.

**Glossary**

*Alternate interpretation*: This building block skill involves helping the client generate an alternate interpretation of his or her experience.

*Brainstorming*: This is a skill that originated in the advertising world to generate ideas in a group environment. It involves a free flow of ideas with an emphasis on quantity and creativity.

*Freewheeling*: Freewheeling is one of the rules for brainstorming. This means that ideas are not judged at the time they are generated. Practical considerations are put off until later. This allows for a free flowing atmosphere where creative and unusual solutions can emerge.

*Challenging Assumptions*: Challenging assumptions is a first step in brainstorming. It involves questioning the limiting ideas that a client brings to the solution of a problem.

*Giving Information*: Supplying data or facts to help the client attain his or her goals. It is recommended that this skill be used sparingly. It may be appropriate for correcting erroneous ideas around parenting, sexuality or drug use, or to provide information regarding accessing social services.

**Exercise 12A: Brainstorming**

The video segment entitled *Reflecting Meaning II* shows a conversation between Dayle, the helper, and Eve, her client. Use this segment to think about the brainstorming process.

a. Step one in brainstorming is to ask yourself, "What is the real problem?" rather than focusing on the proposed solution. In this case, Eve's proposed solution is to move back home. As you watch the segment, what do you think Eve is really hoping to achieve? In other words, what is her real problem?

_____

_____

b. Using the real problem above, brainstorm 10 different solutions to this concern. Remember to be open to unusual ideas and not censor your ideas as they come up. Don't judge them as to their practicality.

_____

_____

c. Now use your analytic faculties and employ the "reality" criterion. Which of these do you think would actually be practical and possible solutions that Eve might consider?

_____

_____

d. Why do you think that Eve has not considered any other alternatives?

_____

_____

Under what circumstances do you think brainstorming is effective? When is it less desirable?

_____

_____

_____

_____

**Written Exercises**
**Exercise 12B: Alternate Interpretation**
Practice creating alternate interpretations to the client statements below. The goal is not to find the correct interpretation, but instead to let the client know there are other possible, more hopeful, interpretations of the events.

1. Client: "This morning I burnt the toast, broke a cup, and then car wouldn't start. This is the beginning of a lousy week."

   Alternate Interpretation:

2. Client: "He didn't call me when he said he would. He doesn't love me."

   Alternate Interpretation:

3. Client: "I had a panic attack yesterday. I thought things were getting better and I was getting over this problem. The anxiety is never going away."

   Alternate Interpretation:

4. Client: "I failed the exam. My father was right, I am stupid."

   Alternate Interpretation:

5. Client: "My wife found out I lied to her. I will never be forgiven for this. She will probably divorce me."

   Alternate Interpretation:

6. Client: "The new guy at work seems so efficient and intelligent. I'll never get that promotion now."

   Alternate Interpretation:

7.  Client: "Monica looked at me today. She probably wants to go out with me."

    Alternate Interpretation:


8.  Client: "My Dad left when I was 6 years old.  Everyone says I was a difficult child. I think that had something to do with my parents divorce."

    Alternate Interpretation:


**Exercise 12C: Giving Information**
Helpers regularly give clients information about other sources of help. They refer clients to agencies and to other individuals who have specialized services or knowledge. Review the following list of typical referrals. See if you can identify someone in your community who delivers these services.

1.  A crisis hotline or 24-hour emergency line_____

2.  A non-profit consumer credit organization that provides help for people with financial problems_____

3.  Parenting classes _____

4.  Help for domestic violence_____

5.  Treatment for substance abuse _____

**Self-Assessment**
Consider the three major building block skills in this chapter.  Indicate any success or difficulty you had in learning each of them, either in the exercises above or in your practice sessions with fellow students.

Brainstorming: (successes and difficulties)

_____

_____


Alternate Interpretation: (successes and difficulties)

_____

_____

Giving Information: (successes and difficulties)

_____

_____

Which of the solution skills presented were most useful or appealing to you? Which of the skills would you feel most comfortable using with clients?

_____

_____

_____

_____

Identify 2 ways you could learn more about, and develop further, the solution skills you noted above.

1.


2.

**Multiple Choice and Short Essay Questions**

1. Which of the following statements is most accurate?
   a. Giving advice makes clients more hopeful.
   b. It is important to give accurate alternate interpretations.
   c. Advice giving is a controversial therapeutic skill.
   d. Helpers should use brainstorming in every session.

2. When may it be appropriate to give advice?
   a. When the helper has limited knowledge in the problem area.
   b. If the client is engaging in unsafe behavior.
   c. When the client looks to others for advice on a frequent basis.
   d. If the client has not heeded previous advice.

3. All of these are "rules" of brainstorming except:
   a. freewheeling is encouraged
   b. quantity is important
   c. do not evaluate suggestions immediately
   d. Place a time limitation on brainstorming sessions

4. List and describe the pitfalls associated with giving advice to clients. Give an example that illustrates a situation where it would be unproductive to give advice to the client.

5. Describe two possible situations where alternative interpretation might be helpful to a client. How could you make a mistake in using this skill?

**Journal**

1. Sometimes clients ask for advice. One interesting technique for dealing with this situation involves asking the client to sit in the helper's chair and give advice to himself or herself. This is a way of tapping in to the wise person in each of us. Think for a moment about your relationships, your family, money, children, or your career. Imagine yourself as this older wiser self and write down some advice to yourself at this stage of your life. Record you reactions to this activity. Do you think this might be a useful technique for working with a client?

2. Begin your journal entry by writing a short poem about your life. It doesn't have to rhyme. The poem should be a picture of your life at this moment in time. Use metaphors to indicate how much effort you are putting forth, how you are dealing with problems and setbacks and how you see your future goals. As you reflect on your poem, did you find that this activity gave you any insight on your present situation? How important is it for you to have a creative outlet in your life? Can you see any value in assigning this activity to a client?

3. Recently, some research has suggested that people who are overly confident do not question their own conclusions and fail to correct their own mistakes. For example, good writers may not critically evaluate their writing or edit it when such a review would actually improve their work. Becoming a reflective practitioner involves carefully examining your own conclusions and looking back on your successes and failures. When reflecting, you are asking yourself to think about how you might improve and consider other ways of viewing the situation. You might even invite the opinions of others. Do you pay enough attention to those things you do well? Do you focus enough on the areas where you need improvement? Can you pay attention to the areas where you need improvement without undermining your self-confidence entirely? Where do you feel most confident and where do you question your abilities at this point in your training?

# Chapter 13
# Outcome Evaluation and Termination Skills

**Chapter Summary**

Chapter 13 in the text emphasizes the need for helpers to utilize assessment tools to determine if helping has been effective. There is a new emphasis on outcome evaluation in schools, hospitals, managed care, and community agencies seeking assurance that clients are making progress towards their goals. In the future, all helpers will need to prove that their helping techniques produce results for the client.

There are a number of easily obtained tools and informal methods for gathering information that will help you determine if your clients are improving. The choice of data that you collect depends on what you and the client are trying to achieve. A traditional data collection process is the progress note in which the helper details changes based on observation and client report. In addition, helpers can employ general outcome measures such as the OQ.45 to detect changes or specific tests for specific problems such as depression, anxiety, or marital satisfaction. Helpers can engage clients in the assessment process by asking them to monitor their own improvement and use subjective measures of discomfort. In addition, the client can enlist the help of a friend or ally to monitor change. Evaluating client satisfaction scales is a way to measure the client's overall happiness with the therapeutic relationship and perceived outcomes. Finally, client and counselor can utilize goal attainment scaling to determine if the agreed upon aims of the helping relationship have been met.

A second issue highlighted in this chapter is dealing with the ending of the therapeutic relationship. There are suggestions about how to know when a client is ready for termination and how to prepare the client for this ending. Both client and helper may experience feelings of loss at this time. Helpers must grapple with their own feelings as they may sometimes resist termination when it is truly in the best interests of the client to deal with life more independently.

The third and final issue in this chapter involves the maintenance stage of the helping process. In other words, how can a helper assist the client in keeping alive the plans and the gains that have been so carefully constructed? Several options are discussed, including the use of fading (reducing sessions gradually), home visits or observation, helping the client to make contact with paraprofessionals, letter writing by the helper, and suggesting self help groups. In addition, the helper can ask the client to engage in self-management and self monitoring activities so that the client can eventually act as his or her own helper.

**Glossary**

*Evidenced based helping*: A recent trend asking for a more scientific approach to treatment selection. Besides monitoring client outcomes, some therapists believe that only empirically proven or supported methods should be utilized.

*Fading*: In this context, fading means reducing the number of sessions over time, finally extending them to three or six month intervals. These booster sessions help maintain gains.

*Goal Attainment Scaling*: A subjective worksheet in which client and helper evaluate the degree to which client goals have been reached.

*Outcome Evaluation*: Outcomes are the desired beneficial effects of helping. The new emphasis on outcome evaluation suggests that helpers need to be focusing their efforts on techniques that work to help clients make progress towards these identified outcomes.

*Progress Notes*: Written records completed by the helper after each session that name the client goals, record client progress towards goals, identify techniques used during the session towards the goal, and future plans and homework.

*Self-help Groups*: Leaderless community groups that help clients maintain gains in areas such as sobriety, weight loss, etc. Examples are Weight Watchers and Alcoholics Anonymous.

*Self-management*: Using behavioral principles to self-reward and self-punish in order to make and maintain desired changes. For example, clients will reward themselves with new clothes if they are able to lose 25 pounds.

*Self-monitoring*: Self-monitoring means that the client is asked to become aware of some behavior or thought and keep records. For example, a client might write down each time during the day when engaging in self-downing thoughts.

*Termination*: Termination is the ending of the helping relationship. This may be done unilaterally when either party is dissatisfied with the outcomes. Positive endings are usually jointly agreed upon when goals are accomplished.

## Exercise 12A: Functional Analysis

One obstacle to change is overcoming the force of habit. A bad habit can be frustrating because we seem to persist in it even when we do not want to. One way of attacking bad habits is to scientifically identify what factors are supporting the behavior. This is called conducting a *functional analysis*. Clients can learn functional analysis and then devise self management strategies to eliminate bad habits by building in rewards (positive reinforcement) for new behaviors. Self management is one of the strategies identified in your text. To understand this process better, select a behavior of your own that you would like to change and follow the instructions below:

1. Begin by identifying the behavior or bad habit you would like to change with as much objectivity, simplicity and specificity as you can. For example, "I bite my fingernails."

---

2. Indicate things that occur simultaneously with or around the same time as the problem behavior, for instance, "I bite my fingernails when I am watching television or when I am reading a good book."

    A.


    B.

C.

3. List things that are consistently not associated with the bad habit. For example: "When I am biting my nails I am not with anyone else."

    A.


    B.


    C.


4. What happens right before the problem behavior?
   Example: "I am nervous."




5. What Happens Right After the Problem Behavior? Do you get a reward or is something negative eliminated?
   Example: "I am angry at myself for biting my nails and I call myself an idiot." (No reinforcer found.)




6. Based on your answers to questions 2, 3, and 4, what are you experiencing when you are doing the problem behavior? In other words, describe, nonjudgmentally, the chain of events. Example: "When I am biting my nails, it seems to distract me and I feel less nervous. Then I engage in negative self-talk."




7. Based on this exercise, what do you think is maintaining (rewarding) the problem behavior? Example: "Biting my nails makes me feel less anxious when I am alone watching television or reading a book."




8. How could you manipulate the environment to reduce the problem behavior?
   Example: "I could make an agreement with myself not to watch television by myself for a

while. When I am reading or watching TV, I could wear gloves. That way, I won't bite my nails without thinking."

9. How could you use rewards to change the behavior?
Example: "If I can make it through one day without biting my nails, I will treat myself to an ice-cream cone. If I can make it through a week, I will go and get a manicure."

10. Devise a plan to manipulate the environment and to reward alternative behavior. Practice your plan on two occasions and note the results below.

Trial Number 1.

Trial Number 2.

- If you feel comfortable discussing your plan with others, involve someone else in your plan so they know what you are trying to accomplish and can support and encourage you (social reinforcement).

- Discuss this homework with your instructor if you are having trouble devising techniques to manipulate the environment or you can't seem to identify suitable rewards.

- When applying these techniques with clients, how will you know which rewards will be the most effective? What kinds of clients and client problems might work best with a functional analysis and positive reinforcement?

**Self-Assessment**
**Assessing Your Progress Toward Your Goals**
We have been discussing client goal attainment and methods for identifying client progress. In this exercise, we will turn this around to help you obtain some evaluation of how far you have progressed on gaining specific helping skills. In the Appendix B, you will find *Table IV: Student Interventions During Session & Evaluation of Depth.* Conduct a practice session (or use your final videotape for this class) that gives you feedback on how much depth you are achieving in 15 interventions. You may use an observer or self-rate as to whether your responses are superficial, maintain the status quo, or deepen the conversation. Write down the entire response

verbatim. The following instructions for the observer are at the top of Table IV in Appendix B and they are repeated here. Judge the responses according to the following criteria:

1) Do the helper's words lead the client to make a more superficial response? Are they judgmental? Do they change the subject or merely fail to respond to the client? If so, make an upward pointing arrow next to that line.
2) The second category of response by the helper is supportive or is a helpful question. This kind of response basically keeps the conversation going. Door openers and minimal encouragers fall in this category. Place a sideways point arrow next to that line.
3) If the helper response reflects unacknowledged feelings or meanings or, in any way, moves the client deeper, place a downward pointing arrow. Tally the number of each kind of arrow.

Now, answer the following questions about your practice session:

1. How many of each type of response does your evaluation show? _____

2. What could you do to reduce the number of superficial (up arrow) responses?

_____

_____

_____

3. How could you increase the number of depth (down arrow) responses?

_____

_____

_____

4. Set a goal for yourself that involves increasing the number of depth responses. Be specific and make sure your target is measurable.

_____

_____

_____

5. If you were a client, how would you feel about being assessed in this way? Would you like to be able to compare your first practice sessions with this one? As a client how do you think you would like having this kind of feedback near the end of your sessions?

_____

_____

**Multiple Choice and Short Essay Questions**

1.  Which of the following refers to using longer and longer periods between sessions as a way of helping the client maintain therapeutic gains following termination?
    a.  self management
    b.  self monitoring
    c.  fading
    d.  spacing

2.  Which of the following can be recommended in preparing a client for termination?
    a.  Discuss termination early
    b.  Make sure client knows how final termination must be
    c.  Downplay the client's feelings of loss
    d.  Use humor to lighten the atmosphere

3.  Outcome evaluation:
    a.  Asks the client what they would like to change
    b.  Is a method only for program evaluation
    c.  Asks us to prove our effectiveness in changing clients
    d.  All of the above

4.  Your client is a 17-year-old high school senior who has been discussing suicidal thoughts with his classmates. What sort of assessment techniques would you use to determine if he or she is making progress? What sort of outcomes would you be tracking?

5.  List and briefly describe each of the methods for maintaining therapeutic gains following treatment.

**Journal**

1.  Have you ever lost an important relationship in your life? Was it someone whom you relied upon for support and advice? If you are able to write about this relationship, answer the following questions: 1) what emotions do you experience when you think about that person? Are you aware of anger, gratitude, or sadness? Do you believe therapeutic relationships could be strong enough to produce this effect? How would you help a client normalize this experience?

2.  Think about a time when you relapsed on a behavior that you really wanted to change. Suppose, for example, you eliminated snack foods and later went back to eating them. How did you feel about yourself after this relapse? Was it hard to get back "on the wagon" after your relapse? Thinking about clients, how can you help them to deal with failure following change?

# Chapter 14
# Curative Factors and Advanced Skills I

**Chapter Summary**

This chapter begins a two-chapter synopsis of the common curative factors of the REPLAN system. The notion of curative factors has been discussed earlier in the book. One of the most potent of these, the therapeutic relationship, is described in Chapter 3. In this chapter, we look at two curative factors in detail: **Enhancing Efficacy and Self-Esteem** and **Practicing New Behaviors.**

Low self-esteem is considered to be a contributing factor to many mental health problems. Consequently, enhancing client efficacy and self-esteem have been traditional goals of the helping professions. In this book, raising self-esteem is described as a curative or therapeutic factor associated with many different techniques. Self-esteem has two aspects: efficacy (or competence) and self-worth (a global sense of worthiness).

*Countering* is a technique helpful in reducing negative self-talk, the "internal critic." For example, an effective counter to the negative belief, "I am unlovable" might be "This relationship just did not work out; I still have a number of people who love me." The process involves assessing negative thoughts by noting both the self-critical statements and associated emotions while identifying the client's main themes and core beliefs. Clients then learn to identify and practice effective contrary statements or *counters.*

Practice is a method for cementing new learning that is acquired in a variety of educational settings. Practice also has many uses in the helping arena. Many treatments for client problems involve exposing the client to new material (see Chapter 15) or teaching him or her new skills. Once these have been learned, practicing the skills during the session and between sessions can speed up the learning process. In this chapter, we discuss two practice methods, role playing and the assignment of homework.

Role-playing is a limited form of psychodrama that has been embraced by a number of other theoretical systems, including behaviorism and gestalt therapy. Role-playing sets up contrived situations and allows the client to try out new behaviors in a safe environment. Role-playing involves three phases: warm-up, action, and a sharing/analysis phase. In the warm-up phase, the client's readiness is enhanced by slowly moving them into the contrived situation. In the action phase, the client produces the target behaviors and may reenact them several times. Finally, in the sharing/analysis phase, the client receives encouragement and feedback from the helper or training group.

A helper uses homework assignments to encourage practice between sessions. Homework demands that clients turn insights into actions. There are a variety of homework assignments to help clients become aware of self-defeating behaviors, to keep a record of practice attempts, and to help clients learn more about their problems (bibliotherapy). Helpers should choose homework assignments that the client is likely to complete successfully. They should be tailored to the specific client and should be simple enough for the client to do without much assistance.

## Glossary

*Aides*: Aides are friends or family who serve as allies to the client in accomplishing a therapeutic goal. Aides supply both help and encouragement. For example, some clients use family members to help them remember to take medication regularly.

*Bibliotherapy*: Bibliotherapy refers to the use of books assigned for the client to read as a method of treatment. Bibliotherapy is a psychoeducational technique.

*Countering*: Countering is a technique that teaches the client to challenge thoughts damaging to self-esteem and replace them with more productive and realistic messages.

*Efficacy*: Efficacy is a component of self-esteem identified by Bandura. It is the expectation that one can perform a specific task; that one is competent.

*Homework*: Homework is out-of-session, *in vivo*, practice by the client.

*Internal critic*: "The voice in one's head" that finds fault and reproaches the self.

*Irrational belief*: Irrational beliefs are Albert Ellis's terms for deeply entrenched, self-destructive ideas about the self. Often developed in childhood, these ideas erode our self-esteem. Examples include "I must be competent in everything" and "I must be approved of by everyone."

*Journaling*: Journaling is a homework assignment in which the client writes about specific topics as a way of solidifying learning. Sometimes journals are used to keep records of improvement in specific client behaviors or in vivo practice.

*Poor body image*: Poor body image is the perception of oneself as physically unattractive and therefore less worthy. A poor body image may cause low self-esteem, and severe problems including unhealthy and dangerous eating patterns.

*Psychoeducational*: Psychoeducational methods are treatments that involve educating a client about psychological issues such as better communication, stress, assertiveness, etc.

*Role-playing*: Role-playing is a technique for recreating past events or enacting future events in a dramatic way. Clients can try out different roles and experiment with different behaviors before in vivo practice.

*Self worth*: Self-worth is one aspect of self-esteem. It is the global feeling that one is good and has a right to exist. It can be summarized as a fundamental belief that one is "OK."

*Warm-up*: Warm-up refers to a client's state of readiness to engage in an activity. Warm-up can be enhanced by mental imagery and role-playing.

**Video Exercises**
**Exercise 14A Identifying Irrational Beliefs**
Irrational beliefs are destructive ideas about the self that damage self-esteem. In Table 11.1 below, each of Ellis's irrational beliefs is paraphrased. Review the video segments indicated and see if you can identify one or two irrational beliefs implicit in the client's story.

Table 11.1
Irrational Beliefs

1. "I must be loved or approved of by nearly every significant person in my life."
2. "I must be completely competent and achieving in all aspects of life to think of myself as a good and successful person."
3. "Some people are bad or wicked and should be blamed and punished for their actions."
4. "It is awful and catastrophic when things are not as I want them to be."
5. "My unhappiness is caused by others and the environment, and I have little or no control over my fear or my negative emotions."
6. "It is easier to avoid problems and responsibilities than to face them."
7. "The past determines my life and I can't escape it. It will continue to determine my future."

a. Review the *Nonjudgmental Listening Sequence* video segment (36:58-43:07) showing the session between Anna (the client) and Mark (the helper).

What irrational ideas can you identify in the client's story?

_____

_____

_____

Construct a "counter" for one of these beliefs by substituting a more rational statement.

_____

_____

_____

b. Review the *Confrontation I* video segment (43:38-47:53), showing the session between Nasundra (the client) and Mark (the helper).

What irrational beliefs can you identify in the client's story?

_____

_____

_____

Construct a "counter" for one of these beliefs by substituting a more rational statement.

_____

_____

_____

c.  Review the *Reflecting Feelings II* video segment (14:00-17:55), showing the session between Lisa (the client) and Mark (the helper).

What irrational ideas can you identify in the client's story?

_____

_____

_____

Construct a "counter" for one of these beliefs by substituting a more rational statement.

_____

_____

_____

**Exercise 14B Identifying Appropriate Practice Activities for Clients**
Although the case studies on the video are brief, try to identify a practice activity that would help the clients in the following videos.

In the *Nonverbal Skills* video segment (beginning at 00:47) the client, Kevin, is dealing with fears associated with an accident. What behaviors does Kevin want to regain?

_____

_____

_____

If you were trying to help Kevin get back to his normal routine, what sort of practice would you suggest (role-play, homework)? Why?

_____

_____

_____

**Self-Assessment**
On a scale from 1-10 (1 = just beginning and 10= mastery) indicate how well you think you have developed the skill of <u>countering</u>. Consider your practice sessions as well as the exercises in this chapter.

1    2    3    4    5    6    7    8    9    10

Now rate yourself on your ability to identify irrational beliefs.

1    2    3    4    5    6    7    8    9    10

Rate yourself on your ability to conduct practice techniques with clients

1    2    3    4    5    6    7    8    9    10

Now rate yourself on your ability to direct a client in a role playing activity:

1    2    3    4    5    6    7    8    9    10

Identify two things you learned while practicing these skills. You may include things that others may have noticed you doing well that indicated your progress. You may also include positive comments from instructors or class members.

1.



2.



Identify two steps you can take to improve your skills further. Identify concrete actions you are willing and able to take.

1._____

_____

_____

2._____

_____

_____

## Multiple Choice and Short Essay Questions

1. Which of the following is <u>not</u> an example of an irrational belief?
    a. I must be thoroughly competent at everything I do.
    b. It is easier to avoid difficulties than to face them.
    c. Things must be exactly as I want them.
    d. I have the right to change my mind.

2. Aides are:
    a. people who assist in a role-play
    b. assistant helpers
    c. books assigned for outside reading
    d. friends or family who help the client practice

3. The expectancy that one can perform a task well is:
    a. self-esteem
    b. self-worth
    c. self-efficacy
    d. self-schema

4. Differentiate between efficacy and self-worth. Is it possible to have one without the other?

5. Discuss the problems associated with assigning homework to clients. Suggest one way of improving client compliance.

**Journal**

1. As you watched the video segments in this chapter, you noted irrational ideas affecting the thinking of these clients. Apparently the clients were unaware that these ideas were affecting their views of the world. Is it possible that we do not even consciously know many of the core beliefs that determine our perspective on life? How can a person become more aware of these ideas? How could you become more aware of your own core beliefs?

2. Some authors have said that self-concept is based on "the reflected appraisals of others." On the other hand, Eleanor Roosevelt believed that no one could make you feel bad about yourself without your permission. Thinking about your own life experiences, which is closest to your opinion on the subject? Are both true for you?

3. The curative factor, Practicing New Behaviors, implies that the helper should encourage the client to act, rather than only talk about, change. It is assumed that changing behavior leads to changes in thinking and feeling. What is your reaction to this idea? In your own life, what have been the most significant catalysts for change? Can you identify any times in your own life when you have tried to face fears, or used action to produce a change?

# Chapter 15
# Curative Factors and Advanced Skills II

**Chapter Summary**

Lowering and Raising Emotional Arousal (L)

Some clients come for the help because they are experiencing excessive emotional arousal. They may be suffering from intense fear, anger, anxiety, or stress. Other clients may have difficulties related to under arousal of feelings. Many clients can benefit to from the quieting techniques of relaxation training and meditation, particularly clients who are experiencing stress and anxiety. Jacobsonian relaxation techniques and diaphragmatic breathing are common therapeutic techniques to reduce bodily stress. Meditation not only reduces anxiety, but quiets the mind and enhances positive emotional states, including joy and optimism. Teaching these skills and instructing clients to use them at home can lower overall emotional arousal.

At the other end of the continuum, emotionally arousing techniques have a long history in the helping professions. Some of the most powerful arousing methods include strong confrontation, psychodrama and Gestalt techniques such as "the empty chair." Methods for raising emotional arousal require the careful assessment and consideration of the client's needs. Due to their potential to hurt as well as heal, these methods are touched on only briefly. In general, only experienced practitioners, within strict, ethical guidelines should use them. In this chapter, we look at two techniques that stimulate emotional arousal and expression: Stimulus Techniques and the Creative Arts.

Activating Client Expectations, Hope and Motivation (A)

Many clients come for help feeling that their situation is hopeless. Many others lack the motivation to achieve goals because they have come at the behest of some third party such as a friend, family member, or the courts. In these circumstances, helpers are called upon to inspire hope, increase expectations, and enhance client motivation. In this chapter, you learn the technique of encouragement. Encouragement means focusing on the positive and changeable, communicating equality and respect for the individuality of the client, pushing the client and lending enthusiasm.

New Learning Experiences (N)

The final curative factor discussed in this chapter is providing the client with New Learning Experiences. Helpers use psychoeducational procedures to teach a variety of new skills such as parenting, marital communication and stress management. Clients learn these through direct instruction as in a classroom. Helpers also help clients develop new perspectives on problems by learning about a new way of looking at the issue. The technique of reframing is one method for changing the client's view of the problem. Helpers use a variety of other methods to transmit new learning to clients including modeling, use of metaphors and stories, humor, asking clients to make changes in the language they use, and exposure to avoided stimuli. This curative factor probably includes the largest number of therapeutic techniques of any curative factor.

## Glossary

*Body scan*: A body scan is a client's internal review of sensations in his or her body from head to toe to identify any areas of tension or disturbance.

*Catharsis*: Catharsis is an experience caused by stimulating emotional arousal and encouraging emotional expression.

*Demoralization hypothesis*: The demoralization hypothesis is Jerome Frank's idea that the primary issues to address in the helping relationship are the client's sense of hopelessness, feelings of incompetence, alienation and loss of self-esteem.

*Diaphragmatic breathing*: This breathing practice consists of inhaling and exhaling below the ribs rather than in the upper chest. Diaphragmatic breathing is used to produce bodily relaxation.

*Discouragement*: Discouragement is Adler's term for demoralization.

*Encouragement*: Encouragement involves helping another person gain faith in himself or herself.

*Expressive techniques*: These techniques help clients fully experience their feelings and express them to the helper. Expressive techniques include the use of stimuli such as books or films to increase emotional arousal and creative techniques such as emotional expression through journaling, drawing and psychodrama.

*Praise*: Praise means positively evaluating another person by giving compliments and noticing progress.

*Psychodrama*: This powerful technique, developed by Moreno, involves the recreation of a scene in the individual's past, present or future to explore his or her thoughts, dreams and emotions as deeply as possible.

*Readiness*: Readiness is a different way of looking at client obstructionism. From this vantage point, clients are not unwilling but unready. Helpers can increase client readiness by educating them, using encouragement and examining the precursors to change that may be lacking in their preparation

*Ventilation fallacy*: The belief that expressing emotions purges them from our system. Current thinking suggests that a cognitive change must accompany emotional expression for maximum therapeutic benefit.

**Exercise 15A: Identifying Levels of Client Motivation**

Use Table 15.1 as a guide and indicate the client's probable level of motivation using Prochaska and DiClemente's model. Classify each response as precontemplation (P), contemplation (C), or action (A). See Appendix A for answers.

1. _____ A client comes to the substance abuse treatment center on three occasions. Each time, he asks questions about the services, but does not wish to make an appointment. He says, "I'll think about it and call you back."

2. _____ A 16-year-old girl comes to her school counselor indicating that she is considering running away to California with her boyfriend. She recognizes the possible legal consequences and her parents' objections, but doesn't want to lose her boyfriend. She has talked to her friends, both about leaving and about staying.

3. _____ A man comes to marriage counseling with his wife because he is having an affair. He wants the marriage to work and will end the affair but claims he should not have to give up his "friendship" with the other person.

4. _____ A couple comes to a school counselor concerning their son's argumentative behavior at school. During the session, the parents squabble and verbally abuse each other. When the school counselor suggests some marriage counseling, the couple indicates that they only want help for their son.

5. _____ A client comes for help to learn better communication skills. He lost his previous job due to poor relationships with co-workers. His present boss has suggested some kind of training because he is encountering the same sorts of problems. Previously, he blamed his co-workers, now he is coming to the realization that the problem lies in the way he talks to people.

Table 15. 1 Prochaska and DiClemente's Stages of Change Model

| Stage of Change | Client Characteristics | Appropriate Techniques |
|---|---|---|
| Pre-contemplation<br><br>de Shazer calls these clients "visitors" | Not even thinking about changing. | Validate that the client does not feel ready to change<br><br>Validate that the decision to change is up to them<br><br>Encourage self-exploration, reading, and gaining information. |
| Contemplation<br><br>de Shazer calls these clients<br><br>"Complainants" | The client is ambivalent about changing. The client is not considering changing within the next month | Encourage clients to weigh the pros and cons<br><br>Help the client think about positive aspects of change and increase expectations. |
| Preparation | The client is testing the waters and is trying to make changes. Client seems to be planning to act within 1 month | Help client identify obstacles to change and help them reduce these obstacles.<br><br>Help client recognize sources of social support<br><br>Assess client to see if they need to learn new skills in order to change.<br><br>Help client make small beginning steps. |
| Action<br><br>de Shazer calls these clients<br><br>"Customers" | Client has made initial steps towards change, has entered a treatment program and has probably been practicing new behaviors for 3-6 months. | Help client recognize times when they are being effective in dealing with obstacles<br><br>Help client avoid environmental issues that will trigger relapse and assist them in dealing with changes in social support group.<br><br>Help client reduce feelings of loss associated with change |

| Maintenance | Client has made a commitment to sustaining new behavior and has been practicing new behavior for 6 months to five years | Plan for follow-up support

Helpers assist clients in identifying support following treatment and also help them recognize the ways they can reward themselves for maintaining change. At the same time, helpers need to bring up the topic of relapse as a normal part of the process. |
|---|---|---|
| Relapse | A relapse is a return to old behaviors. For example, a client begins smoking after a period of five years without tobacco. | Help clients recognize triggers that caused relapse and plan to deal with them.

Help clients become aware of the motivation they possess for change, their present level of motivation and issues that block them.

Help them develop more effective coping strategies. |

**Exercise 15B Identifying client levels of motivation.**
In Table 15.1, two similar viewpoints on client motivation are identified, Prochaska and DiClemente's model and de Shazer's. These models suggest that different helper interventions are appropriate for each level of a client's willingness to change. In the stage of Precontemplation and the Visitor levels, clients do not believe they have a problem and are not thinking about solutions. At the Contemplation or Complainant stage, the client is feeling uncomfortable and thinking about change. At the Preparation stage, the client is dabbling. At the higher stages, the client is ready to take action to change or maintain change.

   Review Table 15.1 and then watch segment entitled, *Confrontation II* (beginning at 48:00) which is an interaction between Dayle, the helper and her client, Catherine. We have looked at this segment previously. This time, let us consider Catherine's level of motivation for change. As you watch, jot down any instances where Catherine indicates her motivation or lack thereof for change. It is clear that she has reasons to stop and other motivations to continue. What are the two sides of the dilemma?

_____

_____

_____

_____

_____

_____

Go back and look at Table 15.1 above and classify Catherine's motivation to stop smoking. Write your conclusion here:

_____

_____

Based on your conclusion, what specific interventions would you recommend for Catherine?

_____

_____

_____

_____

Social support is described as an important catalyst for change. How could Catherine use social support to help her give up smoking (if she decides to quit smoking)?

_____

_____

_____

_____

_____

**Exercise 15C: Learning whether to Quiet or Arouse Emotions**
Review the video segments identified below, and consider whether the client is, in general, over aroused or under aroused emotionally. Would the client benefit more from techniques that arouse or those that quiet emotions?  Give your reasons.

a.  Review the _Reflecting Feelings I_ video segment (10:30-13:58), showing Chris (the helper) working with Margaret (the client). Do you think that Margaret would benefit most from techniques that would raise emotional arousal or lower emotional arousal?

_____

_____

Why?

_____

_____

_____

_____

b. Review the *Nonverbal Skills* video segment (00:47-03:10), showing Chris (the helper) working with Kevin (the client). Do you think that Kevin would benefit most from techniques that would raise emotional arousal or lower emotional arousal?

_____

_____

Why?

_____

_____

_____

_____

c. At 02:20-02:38 (*Nonverbal Skills* segment) the client's emotional arousal appears to have increased. The therapist does not try to increase his emotional arousal; rather she seems to lower it. How did she do this?

_____

_____

_____

_____

**Self-Assessment**
**Using Praise**
Do you tend to use praise in your sessions, saying "Good," and "That's great," when a client makes a positive step? How would you describe your use of praise?

I overuse praise, evaluating the client too much _____

I use praise about the right amount, maybe once during a session _____

I use encouragement rather than praise most of the time _____

I do not use much encouragement or praise at all _____
Ask a classmate to rate you on your use of praise based upon the categories above. Get this information from a recent practice session.

**Multiple Choice and Short Essay Questions**

1. Which of the following describes Prochaska and DiClemente's stage called "Precontemplation"?
   a. the client is not even thinking of the issue as a problem
   b. the client is beginning to think about the problem
   c. the client has relapsed and is in denial
   d. the client is ready to take action.

2. Which of the following statements is <u>not</u> true?
   a. cathartic methods should be used only by experienced practitioners
   b. emotional expression alone may not be sufficient to create change
   c. meditation can reduce anger in clients
   d. relaxation methods should be used with most clients

3. An effective reframing of the client's problem should:
   a. fit the facts as well as the old definition
   b. respect the client's worldview
   c. be more positive and constructive than the old definition
   d. all of the above

4. How does emotional arousal and expression stimulate change? How does reducing emotional arousal help clients?

5. Differentiate between praise and encouragement. Why does encouragement appear to be a better method than praise for dealing with children?

6. List and describe five techniques for changing a client's perspective or perceptions about a problem

**Journal**

1. Reflect on a time in your life when you have been overcome with emotion. How did you cope with these feelings? Did you seek social support? Did you express your feelings or deny them? Did you try and solve the problem that was causing the situation? As you review one or two of these incidents, what would you say is your basic coping style? How do you handle emotional problems automatically? What improvements or new techniques might help you cope better in the future?

2. Think for a moment about a time in your life when you were discouraged and someone offered encouragement. Perhaps it was a teacher, minister or priest, a parent or a friend. How did he or she do this? Was it a long period of time or relatively brief? How much time is really needed to be a source of encouragement to another person? Do you think there is some danger in raising people's hopes?

# Appendix A

**Answers to Multiple Choice and Essay Question and Selected Written Exercises**
**Our Answers to Written Exercises:**
We have provided answers to the written exercises as we would have answered them. Use our answers as a guideline but not as the only answers. If your responses differ significantly, reflect on them and then discuss with your instructor. In some cases, you have discovered an angle we have not considered. At other times, you may be reading more into the scenario than we suggested.

## CHAPTER 1
**Chapter 1: Multiple Choice and Short Essay Questions**
1. a. dualistic
2. c. a person who can do a day's labor unsupervised
3. a. being consistently genuine, in thought, word and deed
4. Essay: Comparing Perry & Trades Model
   - Perry (1970) described 3 stages of development, the dualistic or "right/wrong" stage, the multiplistic stage and the relativistic stage.
   - The skilled trades notion of expertise refers to 7 stages, that of the naivete, novice, initiate, apprentice, journeyman, expert and master.
   - Perry's stages are cognitively based, whilst the trades' notion is more skills oriented.
   - Perry's dualistic stage refers to the absolutist, right/wrong thinking regarding helping responses, the multiplistic stage to the knowing that there is no absolute "right" answer and the relativist stage to the understanding that while many responses are appropriate, some are relatively better than others depending on circumstances.
   - The skilled trades' notion of expertise is the common sense approach. The naivete refers to one who knows nothing of counseling - a lay person, the novice to the new trainee, the initiate to the person accepted to the course or completing introductory training, the apprentice to someone beginning counseling work - perhaps as an assistant, the journeyman to the helper who can work unsupervised for a day, the expert is an exceptional journeyman whose skills are thought highly of by peers; and the master is one of a select few qualified to teach and whose practices become standards.
5. Essay: Recommended helper attitudes are:
   - congruence (the ability to be genuine and consistent in feeling, word and action),
   - positive regard (a belief that all persons are inherently good and worthy of respect),
   - empathy (the ability to understand another person's world, and communicate that understanding)
   - and the courage to confront (the ability to "go for the jugular", and make clients aware of sometimes painful realities).
   - Other attitudes include a positive view of others, good self esteem and mental health, good self-care skills, creativity, intellectual ability, flexibility regarding ambivalence, unfinished business and moral dilemmas, and courage.

## CHAPTER 2
### Exercise 2A: Reasonable and Unreasonable Ideas About Learning the Art of Helping

1. "Everyone learns at his or her own pace, it is an individual process. I will learn some skills more quickly than others. It is not an indicator of my lack of ability as a helper."
2. "The skills of helping are challenging and take a lot of practice. No one learns these skills after one or two attempts. The art of helping is life learning process."
3. "Client progress can take time, and the signs are not immediately obvious. I am focusing on my listening skills and trusting the helping process."
4. "I will not like every client, and that's okay. By challenging my ability to be accepting and non judgmental, this client is offering me an opportunity to look at myself and grow as a helper."
5. "The fact that I am able to perform the skill well at times is an indicator of progress. With more practice I will be able to perform it more frequently and with better timing."

### Chapter 2: Multiple Choice and Short Essay Questions

1. b. assertiveness
2. d. evaluation and termination
3. a. the interviewee may not be helped by the interview.
4. Essay:
   - Maintaining a Strong Client/Helper Relationship. The first stage. Is central to the helping process, supporting all other activities. Through the use of invitational skills, a safe, understanding, supportive environment is created which allows the client to open up.
   - Assessment. The second stage. Is inseparable from relationship building and continues throughout the helping process. Includes the formal and informal ways that helpers collect information about clients
   - 3. Goal-setting. The third stage. The process of drawing up a treatment plan, identifying specific mutually agreed upon goals and the interventions used to achieve them. Often goals are defined behaviorally.
   - 4. Intervention and action. The fourth stage. The process of using more advanced skills to help the client reach their goals, and asking the client to take active steps in this process.
   - 5. Outcome Evaluation and Termination. The fifth stage. The process of regularly asking the client to evaluate and reflect on the progress made toward their goals, and the effectiveness of specific techniques and homework. Toward final sessions in may involve reviewing and celebrating progress. When goals are met decisions are met whether to set new goals or terminate the relationship.
5. Essay:
   - There is no best single answer to this question. Relationship building is most appropriate in the beginning, and practicing new behaviors is certainly a later development. What do you think?

## CHAPTER 3
### Exercise 3B: Identifying Appropriate Helper Self-Disclosure

1. "I've had challenges with bosses. When things are not going well at work, it seems to affect the rest of your life too."

2. "I have lost someone close to me but at the same time, I know grief is a very individual experience. I would like to understand what this has been like for you."
3. "I have had problems with alcohol in the past. I know some of the challenges you are facing."
4. "As I have never been depressed, please help me understand what it feels like for you."
5. "I know what is like to what something badly and how consuming that can be."

**Exercise 3C: Roadblocks Exercise**
1. Answer provided in the text
2. Roadblock Response: "Alcohol use is the wrong way to relax. It causes more problem than it solves."
   Appropriate helper response: "So you enjoy the feeling alcohol provides but have some concerns about using it. Tell me about your concerns."
3. Roadblock Response: "I suggest you run every day and eliminate fats and sugars from your diet."
   Appropriate helper response: "I'm curious about the reasons you have for wanting to lose weight."
4. Roadblock Response: "That seems like a lazy attitude to life."
   Appropriate helper response: "How did you feel about yourself when you made this decision?"
5. Roadblock Response: "This codependent response is probably based on your fear of rejection."
   Appropriate helper response: "What would be the worst part about hurting his feelings?"
6. Roadblock Response: "I'm sure she isn't. She'd be crazy to risk losing you."
   Appropriate helper response: "Tell me some more about the fights."
7. Roadblock Response: "Why do you keep speeding? Can't you stop?"
   Appropriate helper response: "You looked sad when you said that. Is that how you feel?"
8. Roadblock Response: "Just keep smiling and look on the bright side."
   Appropriate helper response: "You feel hopeless about the future right now."

**Chapter 3: Multiple Choice and Short Essay Questions**
1. c. Listening attentively to the client's story
2. a. Empathizing
3. b. A strong client/helper alliance is a good predictor of positive therapeutic outcome.
4. Essay: May include four of the following:
   - The purpose of the relationship is the resolution of the client's issues. It is a one-way street where the helper is the giver.
   - There is a sense of teamwork, as both helper and client work towards a mutually agreed-upon goal.
   - There is a contract specifying what will be disclosed to others outside of the relationship. Safety and trust are established, allowing honest disclosure by the client and feedback from the helper.
   - Unlike a social relationship, secrets will not circulate. As the client experiences this safety, he or she begins to discuss deeper and deeper issues.

- There is an agreement about compensation for the helper. Although some helpers may be volunteers, most receive credit or money for each client hour.
- There is an understanding that the relationship is confined to the counseling sessions and does not overlap into the participants' personal lives.
- As a contractual relationship, the relationship can be terminated.

5. Essay:
   - The helper can appear confident, organized and interested, using verbal and nonverbal cues associated with attentiveness.
   - The helper's office environment can reflect organization, competence and success.
   - Demonstrating skills and abilities ethics, and developing a good reputation in the community and with other professionals.

## CHAPTER 4
### Chapter 4: Multiple Choice and Short Essay Questions

1. a. cultural competency
2. c. The degree of potency granted by the culture to a helper based on age, profession etc
3. d. All of the above
4. Essay:
   - The helper must make every effort to avoid cultural encapsulation by recognizing that for every cultural or socioeconomic difference there is: 1) Knowledge that the helper should possess, 2) Attitudes that will facilitate dealing with someone who is different and 3) Skills that may be helpful in bridging the gap.
5. Essay:
   - Knowing someone's culture is not enough; you must also know the degree to which they are *acculturated*.

## CHAPTER 5
### Exercise 5B: Labeling Opening Skills

1. Encourager: Door opener
2. Encourager: Minimal encourager
3. Door opener
4. Closed question
5. Encourager: Door opener, minimal encourager
6. Encourager: Minimal encourager
7. Open question
8. Closed question
9. Open question

### Exercise 5C: More Practice in Classifying Helper Opening Skills

1. Encourager: Door opener
2. Open question
3. Minimal encourager
4. Encourager: Door opener
5. Closed question

6. Open question
7. Encourager: Minimal encourager
8. Open question
9. "Tell me what you liked about school in Ohio." Open question.

## Exercise 5D: Responding Using Opening Skills
1. "Say some more about this problem."
2. "Go on."
3. "What leads you to believe he feels this way?"
4. "Mmmm"
5. "How do you feel when he acts this way?"
6. "I imagine this is affecting your relationship with your wife."

## Exercise 5E: More Practice Using Opening Skills
- "Tell me about what she wants us to talk about."
- "Okay."
- "How did you see what happened?"
- "Say some more about what happened next."
- "Did anyone get hurt?"

## Chapter 5: Multiple Choice and Short Essay Questions
1. c. How did you get through that experience?
2. c. Closed questions should be used primarily to gain important facts and information.
3. b. body language
4. Essay: Eye Contact
   - make eye contact that it is broken intermittently and naturally.
   - In the west, lack of eye contact may indicate indifference, dishonesty or shame
   - A fixed stare can be disconcerting. In some cultural groups and military organizations, direct eye contact is considered rude, defiant or sign that you consider yourself superior
5. Essay: Open vs. Closed Questions
   - Closed questions ask for specific information and usually require a short factual response.
   - Open questions allow more freedom of expression and typically elicit a longer and broader response.
   - Closed questions are important to get certain facts straight, but they tend to interrupt the client and are less productive.
   - Open questions tend to open the client up and are preferable, in general, to closed questions in the helping setting.

## CHAPTER 6
### Exercise 6B: The Skill of Paraphrasing: Reflecting Content
1. "His behavior seems to have worsened and you don't know how help."
2. "Your dismissal was sudden and doesn't make much sense to you."
3. "You believe your mother-in-law bought these gifts, knowing your views about them."
4. "You think it was unfair you got in trouble with the teacher."
5. "This financial loss has caused you to doubt whether you can fulfill your dreams."

**Exercise 6C: Making Your Paraphrases Nonjudgmental**

1. "Your doctor thinks you should leave your husband because he is violent and you are uncertain whether you want to do this, partly because you think he is not totally to blame for his actions."
2. "You have plans to marry someone you have very strong feelings for, that you have yet too meet face to face."
3. "You are facing a big decision that impacts not only your career and your potential to have a family in the future, but the life of a child."

**Chapter 6: Multiple Choice and Short Essay Questions**

1. d. Your mother phones you twice a day.
2. b. It is important that reflections are nonjudgmental.
3. c. In your opinion, Jack is not showing you enough affection.

4. Briefly describe the four functions of reflecting skills in the helping relationship.
   - Reflecting is a verbal way of communicating empathy.
   - Reflecting is a form of feedback or a mirror that enables the person to confirm or correct the impression he or she is giving.
   - Reflecting stimulates further exploration of what the client is experiencing.
   - Reflecting captures important aspects of the client's message that otherwise might remain camouflaged.
5. Identify two common problems in the process of learning to paraphrase in the helping relationship. What techniques or strategies could you use to overcome these challenges?
   - Simply reciting the facts
   - Difficulty hearing the story because of "noise"
   - Worrying about what to say next.
   - Being judgmental and taking the client's side
   - Being judgmental of the client

**CHAPTER 7: Reflecting Skills II: Reflecting Feelings**
**Exercise 7A: Recognizing Paraphrases and Reflections of Feeling**

1. P
2. ROF
3. ROF
4. P
5. ROF
6. ROF
7. P
8. ROF
9. ROF
10. ROF

**Exercise 7E: Identifying Feelings in Client Statements**

1. Guilt, shame, confusion, excitement, disloyalty, loyalty, disappointment, frustration, fear.

2. Anger, resentment, confusion, loyalty, fear, disloyalty, intimidation.
3. Fear, guilt, helplessness, shame, rejection, disappointment.
4. Fear, confusion, powerlessness, frustration.
5. Anxiety, worry, apprehension, intimidation, fear, frustration, disappointment, resentment.

## Exercise 7F: More Practice in Identifying Specific Feelings
1. You feel furious.
2. You feel helpless.
3. You feel amazed, happy
4. You feel extremely disappointed.
5. You feel excited.

## Exercise 7G: Connecting Feelings and a Paraphrase
1. You feel insecure because your girlfriend seems to enjoy his company.
2. You feel frustrated because they don't appear to be supportive of your dreams.
3. You feel betrayed because your trust was broken.
4. You feel afraid because your sister may be in an unhealthy situation.

## Exercise 7H: Keeping the Focus on the Client while Reflecting Feelings
1. You feel intimidated because his behavior is threatening to you.
2. You feel resentful because she seems to put you down.
3. You feel frustrated because you are not getting the respect you want.
4. You feel worried because she looks so sad.
5. You feel rejected because his work seems more important than spending time with you.

## Chapter 7: Multiple Choice and Short Essay Questions
1. d. Your mother phones you twice a day.
2. b. You are confused about which direction to take.
3. c. Reflecting feelings can deepen the helping relationship
4. Discuss the main differences between reflections of feeling and paraphrases. Give an example of each as if you were saying them to a client.
   - Paraphrases are distilled versions of the main thoughts, behaviors and intentions embedded in the client's story, the content.
   - Paraphrases do not respond to feelings. The qualities of effective reflection of feeling may include three of the following
5. Identify and briefly describe 3 qualities of effective reflections of feeling.
   - They are in the form of a statement, not a question.
   - They mirror the client's emotions accurately, whether expressed or unexpressed. The feeling is reflected with the appropriate shade of intensity
   - It is nonjudgmental, taking neither the client's nor a third party's side.
   - They reflect the client's feelings, not a third party's feelings which the client may discuss.
   - They use different words than the client used. Reflections of feelings do not parrot the client's words back to them.
   - They are short and succinct.

# CHAPTER 8

## Exercise 8E: Practice in Reflecting Meaning

1. Question: "What has been the hardest part about losing your friend?"
   Reflection of Meaning: "You feel guilty because you never told him how much you loved him."
2. Question: "What is troubling you about what happened?"
   Reflection of Meaning: "You feel ashamed because you lied and let your parents down."
3. Question: "What hurt the most?"
   Reflection of Meaning: "You feel angry and hurt because in both cases, nobody asked you."
4. Question: "What makes it so hard for man like your self to accept this type of help?"
   Reflection of Meaning: "You feel humiliated because you are not living up to your family's ideas of what a man should be."

## Exercise 8F: Constructing a Nonjudgmental Listening Cycle

1. "Can you tell me about some of the difficulties you are facing in your social studies class?"
2. "You have difficulty getting motivated for this class as you are sleepy, find it boring and don't think you will need it in the future, but your mom thinks its important and wants you to pass."
3. "You feel resentful because of all the pressure on you."
4. "You feel torn because you want to be loyal to each of your parents as well as be "adult" and make decisions to yourself."
5. "You feel very confused about whether or not to give your studies the focus they require. What makes it confusing is that your parents have different views on the subject. You want to please each of them and you want to be independent and make your own decisions. Although you have a number of personal reasons for wanting to pass, you want to be considered an "adult" and doing want your mom wants might be considered a "childish" thing to do."

## Chapter 8: Multiple Choice and Short Essay Questions

1. d. all of the above
2. d. a and b
3. d. all of the above
4. The text identified four different types of summaries. Identify these and explain when each should be used.
   - Focusing summaries are used at the beginning of a session, to bring the discussion back to the major issues and themes, place a spotlight on the client's responsibility for the problem, and remind the client of the goals.
   - Signal summaries are used in the middle of the session to let the client know the helper has digested what has been said and the session can move along.
   - Thematic summaries are used to connect content, emotions, and meanings that are expressed in many client statements.
   - Planning summaries are used often at the end of the session to review progress, plans and agreements.

5. Construct a dialog between a helper and client in which the helper uses the Nonjudgmental Listening Cycle to explore a particular topic.

Helper: "How can I be helpful to you?" (Open question)

Client: "I just feel I can't cope right now, I have so much going on."

Helper: "Go on." (Minimal encourager)

Client: "I am in the process of moving house, I am trying to run a business from home, I am in school full-time and I have a book that needs to be completed by the end of the month."

Helper: "You have so many things happening at once." (Paraphrase)

Client: "I have all these wonderful opportunities, but it feels like I'm never getting on top of things."

Helper: "You sound totally overwhelmed." (Reflection of feeling)

Client: "I am, completely. I feel exhausted all the time, like I'm never getting on top of things"

Helper: "Go on." (Minimal encourager)

Client: "I guess I feel responsible for everything."

Helper: "Help me understand about feeling responsible." (Door opener)

Client: "I feel like I'm letting people down, because I am spread so thin. I am not giving my customers the attention they deserve, I am frustrating my editor, and I am not spending time with my friends and family. I am not there for them right now."

Helper: "You feel guilty that you are not leaving up to others expectations." (Reflection of feeling)

Client: "Exactly. I have to please everyone, and I don't think I can."

Helper: "What would be the worst thing about you not being what they want you be?" (Open question)

Client: "I guess that maybe they might get angry with me, or maybe they might get fed up with me."

Helper: "You feel scared because if you aren't "perfect" you may lose those people that are important to you." (Reflection of meaning)

Client: "I never thought about it like that before, but that sounds kind of true."

Helper: "Though you have many exciting opportunities right now, you are beginning to realize you can't live up to the high expectations you have for yourself. You feel guilty disappointing people, because others' approval is very important to you, in part because you fear their rejection." (Summary)

## CHAPTER 9
### Exercise 9D: Identifying Discrepancies

1. Client says prom is a waste of time (verbal message) vs. doesn't want to disappoint his girlfriend.
   Or
   Client would like to be involved in the music for the prom vs. does not want to face his embarrassment with Robert.
2. Client says she has a good relationship with her boyfriend vs. publicly acts as if she does not have a boyfriend.
   Or
   Client says relationship is not serious vs. she has been dating him for a year.

3. Client is excited by business vs. says that some parts of business are very boring.
Or
Client says he enjoys business vs. finds himself tortured when he has to sit down and study it.
4. Client reports that he and spouse have always gotten along vs. presently feeling very dissatisfied about their relationship.
Or
Client expected to enjoy retirement vs. feeling that he is a problem to his wife and she is a problem to him.
5. Client feels as if he has fulfilled his dreams vs. feeling that he is still not satisfied.
Or
Client feels he should be happy vs. client experiences that he is trying to escape unhappiness via drinking.

## Exercise 9E: Irrational Beliefs Exercise

1. a. I must be thoroughly competent, adequate and achieving in all areas of my life.
   b. I can reasonably expect to be competent and achieving in some areas of life and not others.
   c. On the one hand you want to excel in all areas of your life, but on the other hand, it is more likely that there will be times when you will be unable to do this.
2. a. I must make the right decision or the results will be awful.
   b. I can reasonably expect to make a decision based on the available facts and my best judgment, but not all outcomes are foreseeable.
   c. On the one hand, you want to make the right decisions, but on the other hand, it is more reasonable to expect that you will make the best decision you can and then learn to live with the consequences whatever they may be.
3. a. I must please everyone in my life.
   b. I can reasonably expect that I will disappoint some people and please others no matter what I do.
   c. On the one hand, you want to please people, but on the other hand, it is more reasonable to expect that, at times, you will disappoint them.

## Chapter 9: Multiple Choice and Short Essay Questions

1. c. It decreases our blind spots
2. b. It is delivered more as a hint than a direct statement.
3. b. A state of internal conflict caused by inconsistent thoughts.
4. Helper behaviors that are most likely to lead to acceptance of a confrontation include:
   a. The development of a strong helper/client relationship prior to confrontation
   b. Helper should develop trust with the client
   c. Confrontations based on too little information are unlikely to be effective
   d. If the issue has been raised on several occasions, the client is more likely to
   e. accept it.
   f. The confrontation should not blame, humiliate or damage client's self-esteem.
   g. Should respect the client's cultural and social values.
   h. Most effective confrontations are well timed, direct, urge the client to act and are

i.  delivered in a caring manner.
j.  The client may agree to resolve the inconsistency. It is more likely to be accepte
    if new goals or agreements are made.
k.  You can tell when a confrontation has not been accepted; the client changes the
    subject, discredits the helper or the helper's comments or falsely accepts the
    confrontation.

5. Steps in Confrontation

   ***Step 1*** Listen carefully and make sure the relationship is well established before con
   Use the nonjudgmental listening cycle to fully understand the client's message and r
   feeling and meaning. Ask yourself if the timing is right or if a confrontation will pre
   place stress on the relationship. Have you earned the right to confront?

   ***Step 2*** Present the challenge in a way that the client will most likely accept it.

   ***Step 3*** Observe the client's response to the confrontation. Determine if the client acc
   partially accepts or rejects the confrontation.

   ***Step 4*** Follow up the confrontation by rephrasing or retreating. When the client does
   accept or rejects the confrontation outright, the helper should try another tack. Becau
   clients often respond to confrontation either by denial or by superficial agreement, th
   must be ready to follow up with additional exploration, another confrontation, or
   clarification.

**CHAPTER 10**
**Exercise 10A: Using Questions for Assessment**
a.  How many cigarettes do you smoke daily?  (obtain a baseline)
b.  Is your target to completely quit smoking?  (clarify the goal)
c.  Have you ever tried to quit before?  If so, how did you do it? (attempted solutions)

**Exercise 10B: Constructing a Genogram**:

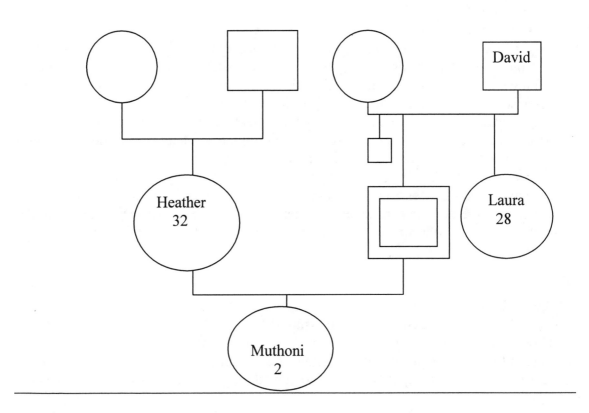

**Exercise 10C: "In Basket" - "Out Basket" Exercise**
Our Answers:

| In Basket | Out Basket (priority ordered) |
|---|---|
| 1. Improve relationship with children | Maintain sobriety |
| 2. Maintain sobriety | Combat feelings of depression |
| 3. Combat feelings of depression | Improve relationships with children |
| 4. Improve work relationship or explore new job | Improve work relationship etc. |
| 5. Engage in creative activities more often | Increase social contacts |
| 6. Increase social contacts | Engage in creative activities |

Indicate why you gave Out Basket item #1 the highest priority.
- This seems pivotal to maintaining the client's present adjustment including work and relationships

Which issues, if improved might have a generalized positive effect on the other areas of life? Should these be elevated on the list?
- Combating depression
- Maintaining sobriety

## Chapter 10: Multiple Choice and Short Essay Questions

1.  c.  a helper's tendency to see things through his or her own cultural lens
2.  d.  all of the above
3.  b.  way of simplifying all of the incoming information about the client
4.  Identify five reasons for spending time in the assessment phase of helping before setting goals with a client.
    -   Assessment gives crucial information to plan useful and realistic goals.
    -   Assessment helps you recognize the uniqueness of individuals.
    -   Assessment uncovers the potential for violence.
    -   Assessment reveals critical historical data.
    -   Assessment can highlight strengths
    -   Assessment can help clients become aware of important problems.
5.  Asking too many questions can be an error. When are questions helpful and when do they hinder?
    -   They hinder during the relationship building stage
    -   They hinder when overused or timing is poor
    -   They can help to signal a change to the assessment stage
    -   In the assessment stage, they are important to get information for genograms, histories, etc.
    -   Questions can stimulate thinking and action
    -   Can help clients focus on goals
6.  List and describe five areas of a client's life you might assess using a genogram.
    -   Cultural and ethnic influences
    -   Alliances and bad feelings among family members
    -   Household composition, previous marriages
    -   Family disturbances affecting the client
    -   Sex-role and family expectations
    -   Economic and emotional support resources
    -   Repeated patterns in client's relationships
    -   Effects of birth order and sibling rivalry
    -   Family attitudes concerning health and illness
    -   Extra-familial sources of support
    -   Family patters preferences, values and beliefs
    -   Document historical traumas
    -   Identify problem relationships

## CHAPTER 11
### Exercise 11E: Focusing on the client

1.  You are worried about the children's welfare
2.  You're angry at your family because you think they stand in the way of your happiness
3.  You resent having to be the one to clean up this mess.
4.  It must hurt to feel excluded from the social life at work.
5.  You feel unappreciated.
6.  What is your response to your mother when she acts this way?

7. Tell me about some of the problems you are facing
8. You're mad and blame the teacher for what's happened.
9. These memories are still difficult for you to deal with.
10. You are concerned about your child and confused about to handle him without help.

**Exercise 11F: Identifying Constructive Goals**
Items 2, 3, 6, 9, 10, 12, and 13 are constructive goals.
1. I want to learn to love myself.
*2. I want to develop two new friendships.
*3. I will take better care of my body by exercising three times per week and eating nutritional foods.
4. My husband will speak to me nicely.
5. I want more self-esteem.
*6. I want to set limits and consequences with my children at least 80% of the time they misbehave.
7. I want to be happier.
8. I want to attend counseling for three sessions to get my probation officer off my back.
*9. I want to ask a woman out on a date.
*10. My family criticizes me and I want them to stop.
11. I want to stop my brother from using drugs.
*12. I want to resolve conflict with my spouse in a new way, without name-calling.
*13. I will to learn relaxation strategies so I can speak in public without shaking.
14. I want to persuade my ex-girlfriend to come back to me.
15. I know I have a drug problem, but I want to get myself squared away financially first.

**Chapter 11: Multiple Choice and Short Essay Questions**
1. d. Constructive goals focus on the client rather than others.
2. b. I will engage in social activities with friends at least twice a week.
3. b. You feel inadequate when you are criticized by your boss.
4. Outline three reasons why goal setting is an important aspect of the helping relationship.
   - Can determine if the client possesses requisite skills or if a referral is needed
   - Imagining success helps make goals easier to achieve. Acquisition of positives (learning skills) is preferable to eliminating behavior.
   - Provides a rational basis for selecting treatment strategies
   - Specific goals reassure us that helping will result in measurable changes
   - Specific goals allow helpers to see how much help the client has received.
5. Briefly describe the characteristics of constructive goals.
   - Should be stated positively
   - Focus on the presence of something vs. absence of something
   - Goals should be simple
   - Goals should be important to the client
   - Constructive goals are realistic

## CHAPTER 12
### Exercise 12B Alternate Interpretation
1. Client: "This morning I burnt the toast, broke a cup and then car wouldn't start. This is the beginning of a lousy week."
   a. It is unusual for so many things to go wrong at once, maybe I have gotten them all the bad luck out of the way.
   b. Tomorrow should be easier than today
   c. These are all small things, not life threatening!
2. Client: "He didn't call me when he said he would. He doesn't love me."
   a. He is forgetful at times, but he has been loving in many other ways.
   b. Something might have come up.
   c. My happiness doesn't depend on one person calling, it's not that serious.
3. Client: "I had a panic attack yesterday. I thought things were getting better and I was getting over this problem. The anxiety is never going away."
   a. panic attacks are going to come and go
   b. I can survive panic attacks
   c. Panic attacks, in general, are reducing in number and strength
4. Client: "I failed the exam. My father was right, I am stupid."
   a. Perhaps failure was due to not studying or not seeking help when not knowing the answer
   b. Perhaps this subject is harder than I thought, I should devote more time.
   c. This is a wake up call to find out where I am having difficulties.
5. Client: "My wife found out I lied to her. I will never be forgiven for this. She will probably divorce me."
   a. This is a serious problem but we have had serious problems before and worked them out.
   b. This is an opportunity for me to look at my dishonesty
6. Client: "The new guy at work seems so efficient and intelligent. I'll never get that promotion now."
   a. I have as many strengths as a worker. I have also been at the company a long time. The promotion board will consider all these factors.
   b. My worth as a person is not dependent on my competition at work.
7. Client: "Monica looked at me today. She probably wants to go out with me."
   a. Monica is a friendly person and her smile is not necessarily a sign that she is interested in me romantically. I need to get to know her better before I can make this assumption.
8. Client: "My Dad left when I was 6 years old. Everyone says I was a difficult child. I think that had something to do with my parents divorce."
   According to what I heard, my parents had a lot of arguments, not just about me.
   a. Having a difficult child is not necessarily a reason to get a divorce.
   b. People rarely share the real reasons for their divorces.

### Chapter 12: Multiple Choice and Short Essay Questions
1. a. Advice giving is a controversial therapeutic skill.
2. c. If the client is engaging in unsafe behavior.
3. d. Place a time limitation on brainstorming sessions

4. List and describe the pitfalls associated with giving advice to clients. Give an example that illustrates a situation where it would be unproductive to give advice to the client.
   - Family and friends can give advice
   - Giving the same advice reflects poorly on the helper
   - Client's frequently do not follow advice
   - They respond with "yes, but…"
   - The helper may become frustrated when the advice is not accepted
   - If the advice is accepted, the helper is responsible, not empowering client
   - Client may come to rely on the helper
   - Advice may violate culture or religion.

5. Describe two possible situations where alternate interpretation might be helpful to a client. How could you make a mistake in using this skill?
   - A client who has low self-esteem and interprets seemingly minor gestures in others as signs that he is being rejected
   - A client who worries obsessively that harm might come to his child.
   - The skill of alternate interpretation can be overused when the client is drawing healthy conclusions about a situation and starts supplying negative alternatives.


## CHAPTER 13
## Chapter 13: Multiple Choice and Short Essay Questions
1. c. fading
2. a. Discuss termination early
3. c. Asks us to prove our effectiveness in changing clients

4. Your client is a 17 year old high school senior who has been discussing suicidal thoughts with his classmates. What sort of assessment techniques would you use to determine if he or she is making progress? What sort of outcomes would you be tracking?
   Assessment:
   - Direct questioning as to the client's intentions  (interviewing)
   - Previous suicide attempts (take history)
   - The use of a suicide potential scale (specific scale)
   - A depression inventory (specific scale)
   - A scale of overall distress (global scale)
   - Look at grades (global scale)

   Outcomes:  Improved grades, decrease reported suicidal thoughts, decreased depression, decrease in overall distress, no suicide attempts.

5. List and briefly describe each of the methods for maintaining therapeutic gains following treatment.
   - the use of fading (reducing sessions gradually),
   - home visits or observation,
   - helping the client to make contact with paraprofessionals,
   - letter writing by the helper and suggesting self help groups.
   - self-management and self monitoring activities so that the client can eventually act as his or her own helper.

# CHAPTER 14
## Chapter 14: Multiple Choice and Short Essay Questions
1. c. I have the right to change my mind
2. d. friends or family who help the client practice
3. c. self-efficacy
4. Differentiate between efficacy and self-worth. Is it possible to have one without the other?
   - Efficacy is the expectancy you will perform a specific task well.
   - Self-worth is a global attitude about your worthiness as a person.
   - It is possible to have one without the other. Many people with low self-worth can identify several areas where they feel efficacious. They may devalue them and separate it from their worth. It is also possible to have self-worth without feeling efficacious in all areas. Perhaps one must feel efficacy in some area to maintain self-worth.
5. What problems and precautions does the textbook identify when assigning homework?
   - Homework assignments that have a high probability of success should be chosen
   - Homework strategies should be individually tailored for each client
   - Regularity of practice is important.
   - Homework should be simple and fit easily into the lifestyle of the client.
   - As the client progresses, homework should increase in difficulty or discomfort.

# CHAPTER 15
## Exercise 15A: Identifying Levels of Client Motivation
1. Contemplation or Preparation
2. Contemplation or Preparation
3. Contemplation
4. Precontemplation
5. Contemplation

## Chapter 15: Multiple Choice and Short Essay Questions
1. a. the client is not even thinking of the issue as a problem
2. d. relaxation methods should be used with most clients
3. d. all of the above
4. How does emotional arousal and expression stimulate change? How does reducing emotional arousal help clients?
   - Can facilitate greater self-understanding and convince client important issues are being dealt with
   - Client experiences acceptance from the helper, increasing self-acceptance, reducing shame, strengthening the relationship
   - Client's attitudes are more susceptible to change right after emotional arousal
   - Reducing arousal can have an impact on mental and physical health.
5. Differentiate between praise and encouragement. Why does encouragement appear to be a better method than praise for dealing with children?
   - Encouragement fosters hope, focuses on intentions and provides support
   - Praise focuses on a specific behavior
   - Encouragement focuses on autonomy, self-reliance and cooperation

- Praise has an external locus of control, encouragement is internal
- Praise can make the client, adult or child, feel that he or she is being judged.
- Encouragement is more democratic, fostering equality and respect

# Appendix B

Table 1.  The Nonjudgmental Listening Cycle

Table 2. Video Evaluation and Student Feedback Form

Table 3. Ten Point Rubric for Evaluating Reflecting, Advanced
Reflecting, Challenging, and Goal-setting Skills

Table 4. Student Interventions During Session & Evaluation of Depth

**Table 1.  The Nonjudgmental Listening Cycle**

1. Open Questions                          "Tell me more about the accident."

2. Encouragers
   a. Minimal Encouragers                  "Okay,"  "Uh Huh,"  "Yes"

   b.  Door Openers                        "Can you tell me more about that?"

3. Closed Questions (important facts)      "How badly were you hurt"

4. Paraphrase                              "So you had to be in the rehabilitation center for several weeks and you're still unable to work."

5. Reflection of feeling                   "You're really embarrassed about what has happened and a little afraid people are blaming you."

6. Reflection of meaning                   "Your identity has always been tied up with your job. Now that you can not work for several months, it is hard to feel good about yourself."

7. Summary                                 "Though you're recovering on a physical level, there are several issues that continue to worry you including how you might perform your job and how other people will see you"

**Table 2: Video Evaluation and Student Feedback Form: Building Blocks**

**Make additional copies of this sheet for practice sessions (2 pages)**

Student_____ Evaluator_____Date: ___/_____/___

| Skill Category | Skill | Number Used During Session (Tally Marks) | Overusing or Not Using This Skill? | Accuracy |
|---|---|---|---|---|
| Invitational (nonverbal) | Eye contact | | | |
| | Body position | | | |
| | Silence | | | |
| | Voice tone | | | |
| | Gestures | | | |
| Opening Skills | Door openers | | | |
| | Minimal encouragers | | | |
| | Open questions | | | |
| | Closed question | | | |
| Reflecting | Paraphrasing | | | |
| | Reflecting Feelings | | | |
| Advanced Reflecting | Reflecting Meaning | | | |
| | Summarizing | | | |
| Challenging | Feedback | | | |
| | Confrontation | | | |
| Goal Setting | Focusing on the client | | | |
| | Boiling Down the Problem | | | |
| Solution Skills | Giving Information | | | |
| | Brainstorming | | | |
| | Alternate Interpretation | | | |

Additional Questions to Evaluate a Practice Session

How able was the student to produce exploration or action on the part of the student?

1    2    3    4    5    6    7    8    9    10

The client rehashed                        The client explored more deeply
old issues                              and covered new ground.

1    2    3    4    5    6    7    8    9    10
The client was                          The client was challenged
Not confronted or                      to act.
Challenged to take action

**Some Key Interventions by the Helper**: (write down as close to verbatim as possible)

_____

_____

_____

_____

_____

_____

_____

_____

_____

## Table 3: Ten Point Rubric for Evaluating Reflecting, Advanced Reflecting, Challenging, and Goal-setting Skills

**A   9.5-10 Surpasses skill level required.  Shows evidence of mastery**
At this level the student is listening to the client using reflecting and advanced reflecting skills appropriately. In addition, the client is urged to explore more deeply by the use of challenging and to act through the use of goal setting skills.

**A- 9.0 Consistently shows skills required but not mastery**
At this level, the student is consistently reflecting feelings and occasionally reflects meaning and paraphrases when needed. The student is listening and responds to the client's message by moving the client to deeper levels.

**B+  8.5 Above average ability to perform required skills**
Students at this level are listening and several times during the interview make responses that are accurate reflections of feeling and meaning but do not push the client to examine deeper levels consistently.

**B   8 Shows average ability to perform the required skills**
Students at this level are listening and using minimal encouragers with occasional paraphrasing and perhaps a few reflections of feeling. At this stage, the student has not yet established regular reflections of feeling or meaning.  Paraphrases outnumber reflections of feeling and meaning combined.

**B-  7.5 Developing skills but not yet performing them consistently**
Students at this level are listening but are not usually intervening to help the client explore more deeply with consistent use of paraphrasing, reflection of feelings or meanings. Helper is usually too silent and uses too many minimal encouragers rather than risking a reflection.

**C+  7.0 Shows some evidence of skills but mostly detracting behaviors**
Students at this level are not listening but merely waiting for the client to stop talking so that they can intervene. Excessive use of questions. A student at this level is not responding to the last client statement but changes the focus rather than asking the client to stay on topic. Detracting behaviors include personal opinions by the helper, roadblocks, advice giving and an excess use of closed questions.

**C   6.5 Unable to perform skills at the required level, detracting behaviors**
present.

**D   6.0 Shows no evidence of  required skills and shows mostly detracting**
    **behaviors.**

# Table 4:  Student Interventions During Session & Evaluation of Depth

## Make additional copies of this sheet for practice sessions.

This is another option for evaluating a practice session, giving feedback as to the *depth* of the helper's responses. After writing down the helper's words, the observer considers the following:  1) Do the helper's words lead the client to make a more superficial response, are judgmental, change the subject or merely fail to respond to the client? If so, **make an upward pointing arrow** next to that line.  If the response by the helper is supportive, is a useful question and basically keeps the conversation going, place a **sideways point arrow next to that line**. If the helper response reflects unacknowledged feelings or meanings or in any way moves the client deeper, **place a downward pointing arrow.** Tally the number of each kind of arrow.

Helper's words as close to verbatim as possible                                                    Depth

_____

_____

_____

_____

_____

_____

_____

_____

_____

_____

_____

_____

_____

                                                                                Tally: